TRUEBLINKA

Adam Rapp

BROADWAY PLAY PUBLISHING INC
224 E 62nd St, NY, NY 10065
www.broadwayplaypub.com
info@broadwayplaypub.com

TRUEBLINKA
© Copyright 2008 by Adam Rapp

1st printing: May 2008, 2nd printing: February 2010
I S B N: 978-0-88145-334-8

Book design: Marie Donovan
Word processing: Microsoft Word
Typographic controls: Ventura Publisher
Typeface: Palatino
Printed and bound in the U S A

TRUEBLINKA originally received a workshop production at the 1997 National Playwrights Conference at the Eugene O'Neill Theater Center (Lloyd Richards, Artistic Director) directed by Israel Hicks. The play was awarded the Herbert & Patricia Brodkin Scholarship.

The world premiere production opened 28 September, Off-Off Broadway, at the Maverick Theater with Last Minute Productions. The cast and creative contributors were:

AVIS . . . . Matthew Stadelmann
EPHESIA . . . . .Gretchen Cleevely
AMOS . . . . .Michael Gladis
RILTHE . . . . Barbara Eda-Young
SMALLWOOD .Andrew Garman
SLOAN . . . . Guy Boyd
CHICK . . . . .Pauline Boy

Director . . . . Simon Hammerstein
Sets . . . . John Conners
Lights . . . . David Zeffren
Costumes . . . . Martin Lopez
Sound . . . . Todd Polenberg
Original music . . . . .Shara Worden

CHARACTERS

Avis
Ephesia
Amos
Rilthe
Smallwood
Sloan
Chick

Time: the present

Place: a small town in the American heartland

ACT ONE

Scene One

(Interior of an old Victorian house. A living room and dining area. Wood floors. Dark, hard-wood furniture. A large oval dining room table. A black medical bag rests at the edge of the table. Two church pews line the table on either side. At first glance the space might resemble a rectory. An old-fashioned phonograph. A door that leads to a bedroom.)

(A prodigious wooden staircase distinguishes the two rooms, but does not intersect them. The walls are bare except for a small collection of Jesus Christ portraits that vary in profile and facial anguish, and ceramic Stations of the Cross. A large flip-style worker's calendar on a wall with days crossed off and tally marks in the margins. Next to the calendar is an enormous industrial clock. A large stained-glass window in the living room casts cathedral-like light. Somewhere in the house there is a low rumbling sound, like that of a furnace.)

(In the living room there is an old sofa, a matching love seat, a wooden rocking chair, a large rope-style throw rug, and a coffee table. There is no T V. A few inclined wooden tables have been set up at the threshold of the living room.)

(At different times during the course of the play, characters appear in front of the kiln, which is in the basement. The kiln emits a harsh orange glow and intense heat.)

(AVIS, eleven, small and thin for his age, is polishing the surfaces of the wooden display tables, while his sister, EPHESIA, thirteen, carefully wipes down stacks of ceramic

crosses. They both wear white T-shirts, blue worker's trousers, white aprons, and black industrial shoes. Their extreme pallor suggests lack of exposure to the sun. EPHESIA's hair is tightly pulled back. She wears no makeup. Their hands appear to be sore and they handle the crosses carefully. They work meticulously, with an almost military-like precision. They work silently.)

(RILTHE, their mother, early-fifties, thickly breasted from child-bearing and hardened in a way that might be likened to an armed services veteran, is setting the table in the dining room. She wears a navy blue denim dress with an apron. Her hair is severely pulled back. Her movements are efficient and angular. She exits to and enters from the kitchen with plates of cheese and crackers. She arranges them carefully and returns to the kitchen, softly singing a church hymn.)

(AMOS, the oldest child, late-twenties, appears out of the shadows with another stack of crosses. There is a narrow, affectless, stoic quality about him. He wears navy blue worker's trousers, a non-descript, matching navy blue collared shirt, and black, industrial boots. Attached to his belt, there is a utility knife sheathed in a leather snap pouch and a large key leash. He carries a clipboard. Through his belt loop he also carries a six-inch blunt-ended wooden pin fashioned from the end of a broom handle.)

(AMOS watches AVIS and EPHESIA, sets a new stack down, grabs a cross from off the table and examines it. After a moment, he hands it back to EPHESIA, points to a small spot, and she wipes it with her cloth. He re-examines the cross and places it back on the display table. RILTHE enters.)

RILTHE: For God's sake let's put a little effort into it.

AMOS: You heard her.

RILTHE: My sloth detector's about to start cawing like a crow.

AMOS: Keep 'em even.

RILTHE: And if Mister Smallwood sees those simple looks on your faces he's liable to turn right around and get back in his Holy Van. Check your work, Avis. *(She exits.)*

AMOS: Check your work, little man.

(RILTHE returns with a plate of meats.)

RILTHE: There is no place for the insignificant in this house. Amos, let's pick up the pace.

AMOS: Pick it up.

RILTHE: The day seems to have gotten away from us. First the bankers with their threats. The decency of vultures.

AMOS: Shouldn'ta let em in.

RILTHE: Ephesia, your work lacks passion. And the words they use. *Conclude. Terminate. Foreclose.* As if they're playing some sort of board game. And their haircuts. All that greasy tonic on their collars. You'd think they were sleeping with Negroes. Avis, your work lacks velocity. *(To AMOS)* Yapping at you in their little gray money suits. Yapping and flapping like pigeons pecking through the debris. Threatening our home.

AMOS: I shoulda chased em.

RILTHE: And they always come in threes. Pigeon suits in triplicate. Like some bureaucratic triumvirate.

AMOS: Next time I'll use the shovel.

RILTHE: What do they need three for?

AMOS: Jewsuits always travel in threes.

RILTHE: One to yap about the mortgage, one to look important, and the other to turn you upside down and shake the coins out of your pockets. Ephesia, help me with this meat.

(EPHESIA *crosses to the meat tray and helps* RILTHE.)

RILTHE: Circumcised heathens. *(Grabs the black medical bag, hands it to* AMOS*)* Take this out of here.

*(*AMOS *exits with the black medical bag.)*

RILTHE: And they walk so delicately. With their little watch chains tapping. Tappety-tap. "No I'm sorry, Mrs Klieg, we *can't* lower the monthly boom; once you're encumbered, you're encumbered. That's why there are dotted lines. That's why things are *notarized* and *certified* and *stamped* and *validated*. That's why my slacks are so *tight*, Mrs Klieg. That's why I'll be performing in soprano this evening." And with all that nasal in their voices. Like everything down low has receded into some gruesome void of genitalia. What happened to the days when men were men?

*(*AMOS *returns angry.)*

RILTHE: Now what?

AMOS: There's bird crap all over hell down there!

EPHESIA: Where!

AMOS: On my boots. On my shovel. On the stokinpoles. On the fuel box! Goddamned ghetto chicken.

EPHESIA: It wasn't a ghetto chicken, it was a pheasant!

RILTHE: It was a filthy and diseased creature. Germs cannot be seen by the naked eye. A virus doesn't make itself known through color or texture. These things do not wave banners. Where are my flowers?

AMOS: They tried cleaning it in my wash pail.

EPHESIA: We were giving it a bath.

AMOS: Wasted my soapstone, too.

EPHESIA: You killed it.

AMOS: I fixed the mess you made.

EPHESIA: It was building a nest and you killed it.

AMOS: It stank.

EPHESIA: It was probably full of babies.

AMOS: Babies with rabies.

EPHESIA: Pheasants don't get rabies.

RILTHE: That's enough! I will not tolerate a melee in here today! I've spent all morning cleaning and purifying and dealing with bankers and preparing for Mister Smallwood's arrival! This nonsense about the bird is over! *(To* AMOS*)* Did you incinerate it like I asked?

AMOS: Burnt to a crip.

RILTHE: Good. What's done is done. Did they sanitize their hands properly?

AMOS: Yes, ma'am.

(She crosses to EPHESIA, *inspects the fronts and backs of her hands.)*

RILTHE: The Duty Clock has numbers for a reason and we are not to challenge their authority.

*(*AVIS *holds his hands out.* RILTHE *crosses to him, inspects his as well.)*

RILTHE: The Negro is late. There's a slowness in his bones. Something flat in the foot. That's why he weakens and develops a thirst for dirty wine and makes his bed at the train station. That's why his spine grows crooked. Amos, tell them to stand up straight. They look like primates.

AMOS: Stand up straight you look like primates.

RILTHE: A couple of chimpanzees. Amos, did you snuff the kiln?

AMOS: Yes, ma'am.

RILTHE: We can't have the breath of hell blasting through the floorboards. Ephesia, did you freshen Mister Smallwood's boutonniere?

EPHESIA: It's in the icebox.

RILTHE: Your hair's a mess.

AMOS: Looks like a shot duck on your head.

EPHESIA: That's cause you keep grabbing it.

RILTHE: When you're finished here you are to go and correct it. If you can't pull it tight enough I will do it for you. Is Chick's refection tray ready?

EPHESIA: I took it to her.

RILTHE: Did she refuse again?

EPHESIA: Most of it.

RILTHE: Lord in heaven.

EPHESIA: She ate the peaches.

AMOS: She's sposed to eat the goddamn liver.

RILTHE: The last thing we need is her howling through the vents while Mister Smallwood is making his selections. Today of all days.

AMOS: Kept me up half the night with her gruntin and groanin.

RILTHE: What did you do with the liver?

EPHESIA: Flushed it.

RILTHE: Flushed it! You don't flush a good meat portion like that!

EPHESIA: The pheasant wouldn't eat it.

RILTHE: The pheasant!

EPHESIA: It was hungry.

RILTHE: You don't feed meat to a fowl! Where's the sense God gave you, Daughter? Next time give it to your little brother. He's weak and he needs the supplement. (*Crossing to* AVIS, *prodding his arms and shoulders*) Weak as a wet paper plate. Where you got it from I'll never know. We have a deformity in the attic and a weakling in the pantry. Who would have thought that the virile blood of your father and the strength of my constitution would have mingled to produce such infirmity. There's a man inside you somewhere.

EPHESIA: I talked to her.

RILTHE: You talked to whom?

EPHESIA: Chick.

RILTHE: You've been told not to enter that room.

EPHESIA: I didn't.

RILTHE: Well, how does one communicate through a wrought iron door?

AMOS: Took four men to haul it up them stairs.

EPHESIA: She talked through the slot.

RILTHE: She can't talk. She doesn't even have a proper mouth.

AMOS: She don't even groan right.

EPHESIA: Her voice is little like a sparrow's.

RILTHE: Well, what did she say?

EPHESIA: She wanted to know if it was snowing yet.

RILTHE: Well, that's rickety. It'll be months before we see snow.

EPHESIA: She said she hoped it had snowed because the ground would be too hard for holes.

AMOS: She can't do nothin but oink and shit like a goddamn sow.

EPHESIA: You're the sow!

AMOS: You're too skinny!

EPHESIA: Assface!

RILTHE: That's enough! Judas Priest! ...And will both of you please stop taking the Lord's name in vain. Enough shenanigans to fill a circus tent. *(To* EPHESIA*)* Had she used the toilet pan?

EPHESIA: Yes, ma'am.

RILTHE: Did she pass a stool?

EPHESIA: Two-and-a-half stools.

RILTHE: Did you note its consistency?

EPHESIA: Dark and supple. It's noted.

RILTHE: Is it properly charted?

EPHESIA: *(Quickly)* She wears a pillow case over her head. She's drawing a face on it. Every day she adds a different part. She said she thinks you're putting something in her food.

RILTHE: Ephesia, I believe I asked you if her stool has been properly charted!

EPHESIA: Yes, ma'am. It's in the books.

RILTHE: And where on earth are my wild asters? I just picked them. *(To* AVIS*)* And you, mister, did you police the driveway?

*(*AVIS *nods.)*

RILTHE: What did you collect?

AVIS: Newspapers.

RILTHE: What else?

AVIS: Some leaves.

RILTHE: That's it?

AVIS: Busted clock. A rope. Coffee can with gum stuck to the bottom. And a hat.

RILTHE: What kind of a hat?

AVIS: A man's hat.

RILTHE: Did you set it on the curb?

(He nods.)

RILTHE: Is it properly bound?

(He nods)

RILTHE: Did you ask the Hobart's to kennel their dog?

(He nods)

RILTHE: I would appreciate it if you would address me once in a while. God put a voice in your throat for a reason.

AMOS: Acts like a goddamn schoolgirl. All quiet and tiny. Should throw a skirt on him and give him some licorice to twirl around his finger.

RILTHE: That's enough, Amos. *(To* AVIS*)* And if you keep picking your face, Avis, you're going to wind up looking like some maladjusted Puerto Rican.

AMOS: Carped him twice for it this morning.

RILTHE: The only times your hands should rise above your shoulders is when, Daughter?

EPHESIA: Eating, praying, or washing.

RILTHE: You hear that?

AVIS: Yes, ma'am.

RILTHE: Mind the clock, now. *(She exits, singing.)*

AMOS: Mind the clock.

EPHESIA: *(Mocking)* Mind the clock.

AMOS: You must wanna get carped, Sister.

EPHESIA: I must.

AMOS: Hussy.

EPHESIA: Pervert.

AMOS: Whore.

EPHESIA: Killer.

(AMOS *produces a long pheasant feather, touches her face with it.)*

AMOS: *(Exiting with a box)* Better fix that hair.

(AVIS *stops suddenly, starts to scratch his groin.)*

EPHESIA: Avis, that's gross!

(AVIS *scratches harder.* EPHESIA *quickly crosses to him, reaches into his pants and pulls out a small, matted arrangement of flowers. She smells them.)*

EPHESIA: You bunkpissed again! And you stole Mother's wild asters!

AVIS: I had to stop the smell.

EPHESIA: So you wash yourself! You must like getting carped.

AVIS: No I don't.

EPHESIA: Why won't you go to the bathroom?

AVIS: The moaning.

EPHESIA: You know it's only Chick!

AVIS: She sounds like a cow. She goes, "*Aaaavis*".

EPHESIA: She probably wants to see you. She's never seen you.

AVIS: I'm not goin up there.

EPHESIA: She's your sister, Avis... Did you burn the sheets?

(He shakes his head)

EPHESIA: Do they stink?

(He nods)

EPHESIA: You have to burn them, Avis. And when you're done take my sheets off my bed.

RILTHE: *(Offstage)* Where are my flowers?

EPHESIA: *(Referring to the wild asters)* And flush these!

AVIS: Did you ask her yet?

EPHESIA: Not yet. But I will, I promise.

(EPHESIA stuffs the flowers back down his pants. AVIS exits up the stairs. RILTHE enters.)

RILTHE: I had a beautiful arrangement of wild asters. I was going to set them on the table.

EPHESIA: I ate em.

RILTHE: You ate them!

EPHESIA: With a piece of lightbread. Flower sandwich.

(A knock at the door.)

RILTHE: *(Quietly furious)* Well, you had better pick me some new ones, daughter.

EPHESIA: Yes, ma'am.

(Another knock)

RILTHE: Now go prepare yourself. And when you greet Mr. Smallwood straighten your carriage.

(EPHESIA pulls her hair tighter and exits to the kitchen. RILTHE starts music on a phonograph. A small church choir sings out. RILTHE crosses to the door, primping.)

(RILTHE *opens the door.* LORENZO SMALLWOOD, *forty-ish, stands in the entrance. He wears a rain slicker, a plain brown suit, a matching fedora hat, and carries a briefcase. He has a pleasant, sincere way about him and smiling eyes. He's the kind of person who can walk into a room and convince strangers to gather around a piano and join him in a sing along.)*

RILTHE: Mister Smallwood?

SMALLWOOD: *(Removing his hat)* Mrs Klieg?

RILTHE: Come in, come in. Welcome.

SMALLWOOD: Thank you.

RILTHE: Let me take your hat and slicker. *(She hangs the hat and slicker on the coat rack.)*

SMALLWOOD: Is that the Vine of Mary growing in the gable?

RILTHE: The very kind.

SMALLWOOD: I had no idea it climbed so high.

RILTHE: It takes a tricky hand.

SMALLWOOD: The Vine of Mary. So green it almost looks blue. I'll be.

RILTHE: Would you like some coffee or tea? Cream soda?

SMALLWOOD: Oh, coffee would be fine.

RILTHE: Milk and sugar?

SMALLWOOD: I take it black, thank you.

RILTHE: Avis?

(AVIS *enters from the staircase.)*

RILTHE: Please get Mister Smallwood a black coffee.

(AVIS *exits to the kitchen.)*

RILTHE: So you found your way okay?

SMALLWOOD: Oh, sure. I know this area like the butcher knows his tenderloin...lovely home.

RILTHE: It's plain but functional.

SMALLWOOD: Isn't that the prettiest window.

RILTHE: Had that installed last spring.

SMALLWOOD: Just divine. Where'd you get it from, if you don't mind me asking?

RILTHE: Saint Rose of Lima auction.

SMALLWOOD: I thought it looked familiar.

RILTHE: Breaks your heart to think of that church closing its doors.

SMALLWOOD: Wasn't it just the saddest affair?

RILTHE: We were happy to acquire a memento.

(SMALLWOOD *crosses to the wall and observes the Stations of the Cross.*)

SMALLWOOD: Saw a set of these over at our Lady of Good Council in Plano.

RILTHE: They're on of our more enthusiastic patrons. I greatly admire their narthex.

SMALLWOOD: And don't they have the loveliest altar? The way the light just floats down from the nave and settles on the tabernacle. Like God has made it rest for a moment.

RILTHE: Oh, and their crucifix is just mighty. The interpretation of Christ is simply heroic.

SMALLWOOD: I helped place that piece, actually.

RILTHE: You did?

SMALLWOOD: Yes ma'am. Took a twelve dollar pot roast and half a bottle of dandelion wine but Father Harold eventually softened up.

RILTHE: Oh, father Harold can be so bullheaded when he wants.

SMALLWOOD: I think he's read the Book of Proverbs one too many times.

RILTHE: Oh, Mister Smallwood.

(They share laughter.)

SMALLWOOD: *(Referring to the music)* Now is that the Shambly Hopelight Choir?

RILTHE: The very ladies.

SMALLWOOD: Saw them in Manteno last Christmas.

RILTHE: At Saint Raymond's on Flunk Street.

SMALLWOOD: Lovely, lovely gals.

RILTHE: My husband and I had planned to go.

SMALLWOOD: Voices of angels. They did a rendition of 'Five Hundred Miles' that would make the sheriff weep.

RILTHE: Oh, we should've gone.

SMALLWOOD: My wife's the one who tipped me off about those Shambly gals.

RILTHE: I'll bet she plays the same collection.

SMALLWOOD: Oh, she's passed on now.

RILTHE: I'm so sorry.

SMALLWOOD: Just this last winter.

RILTHE: Oh, dear.

SMALLWOOD: She was an afflicted woman.

RILTHE: Well God bless you, Mister Smallwood.

(RILTHE *crosses to the phonograph, stops the music.*
AVIS *enters with coffee.*)

SMALLWOOD: And who is this sharp-looking fella?

RILTHE: This is my youngest boy, Avis.

SMALLWOOD: How do you do, son?

(SMALLWOOD *extends his hand.* AVIS *proffers the coffee.*)

RILTHE: Well, answer Mister Smallwood, Avis.

AVIS: Hi.

(AVIS *extends his hand and they shake.* RILTHE *strike's*
AVIS' *arm down and grabs* SMALLWOOD's *hand firmly.*)

RILTHE: Put some authority into it, Avis. *(To*
SMALLWOOD)You'd think he was raised by
homosexuals. *(To* AVIS) Now try it again.

(AVIS *extends his hand. They shake again.*)

SMALLWOOD: *(Faking an injured hand)* Whew. Now
there's a handshake. Nice to meet you, Avis.

AVIS: Nice to meet you.

RILTHE: Avis is learning how to operate the kiln.
Just got a new one with manifold tiers. His brother
Amos has been teaching him.

SMALLWOOD: Takes a strong constitution to manipulate
fire.

RILTHE: Amos worked for the local fire department.
He can make a flame fold over on itself and play dead
if he wants. We're hoping that Avis will develop a
similar aptitude.

SMALLWOOD: I'm sure with a little practice and an eye
for the flame that Avis here'll be stirring up a kiln in no
time.

RILTHE: We hope so.

SMALLWOOD: With daily prayer and knowledge of the Scriptures, the bone thickens and fosters the gift tolerance. *(To* AVIS*)* Would you like to see what's in my pocket?

*(*AVIS *doesn't respond.)*

RILTHE: Well, go on, Avis. We're all friendly here.

*(*SMALLWOOD *exaggerates searching in his pocket and pulls out a plain doughnut.)*

SMALLWOOD: Well, would you look at that! Straight from the Chidy Street Bazaar! *(Handing the doughnut to* AVIS*)* A little holy bread.

RILTHE: What do you say, Avis?

SMALLWOOD: Oh, you don't have to say a thing. You're quite welcome.

*(*AMOS *enters.)*

SMALLWOOD: And this must be Amos.

RILTHE: Amos, this is Mister Smallwood.

SMALLWOOD: Hello, Amos.

(They shake.)

AMOS: Pleased to meet you, Sir.

SMALLWOOD: Likewise.

*(*AMOS *crosses to* AVIS, *stands behind him. They stand very still, their arms behind their backs, almost at parade rest.)*

RILTHE: And I don't know what's keeping their sister. *(Calling out)* Ephesia?

*(*EPHESIA *enters from kitchen, carrying boutonniere. She offers it to* SMALLWOOD.*)*

RILTHE: This is Mister Smallwood. Pay your respects.

EPHESIA: Nice to meet you, Sir.

(EPHESIA *joins her brothers, places her arms behind her back as well.*)

SMALLWOOD: Pleasure's mine. *(Pinning it to his lapel)* Nothing like a flower to make the day bright.

(Suddenly, a loud moaning from somewhere in the house.)

RILTHE: Those darn floorboards. Every fall they get to moaning like a wild hellhound.

(The moaning again. It ceases.)

SMALLWOOD: The dreary cry of the lone hellhound. Release me from this long and hot, sequestered night... *(Referring to the display tables)* Shall we? *(He studies the crosses.)*

RILTHE: Took a month of Sundays to get the glaze right.

(SMALLWOOD continues studying them for a moment.)

SMALLWOOD: What are your thoughts on the cross, Mrs Klieg?

RILTHE: My thoughts?

SMALLWOOD: Your philosophy, as it were.

RILTHE: Well, it's an instrument.

SMALLWOOD: Yes. It is an instrument. It is that indeed. *(Turning and weighing the crosses)* What kind of instrument, exactly?

RILTHE: An instrument of worship.

SMALLWOOD: I spose it could be called that.

RILTHE: And congregation.

SMALLWOOD: Congregation, sure.

RILTHE: A symbol of affliction that tries one's virtue.

SMALLWOOD: That's part of it, Mrs Klieg. Part of it, indeed. You're warmin up.

RILTHE: Well, I'm not sure exactly what kind of answer you're looking for, Mister Smallwood.

SMALLWOOD: Oh, I think you do, Mrs Klieg.

RILTHE: Please, call me Rilthe.

SMALLWOOD: If you'll call me Lorenzo I'll call you anything you'd like.

(RILTHE *laughs. She looks at her children, nods at them and they laugh as well.)*

RILTHE: Would you care for some meat? There's a whole plate of it over on the table.

SMALLWOOD: No, thank you. I'm trying to cut down... So, what do you say, Rilthe? About the cross.

RILTHE: It's a crucifixion tool.

SMALLWOOD: There you go.

RILTHE: For public implementation.

SMALLWOOD: Forfeiture of sin. Earthly relinquishment.

RILTHE: Atonement.

SMALLWOOD: Reparation and oblation.

RILTHE: Sacrifice and immolation.

SMALLWOOD: Consecration. *(Turning the cross in this hand)*The crucifixion or death of Jesus on the cross is recorded in all four gospels, Rilthe. The cross became the symbol of Christ's sacrifice and of the Christian gospel of redemption. Paul declared "Far be it from me to glory—"

RILTHE & HER CHILDREN: "—except in the cross of our Lord Jesus Christ."

SMALLWOOD: Galatians.

RILTHE: Galatians six fourteen.

(SMALLWOOD *sets the cross down.)*

SMALLWOOD: Rilthe, have you ever heard of *The Dream of the Rood*?

RILTHE: No, I can't say that I have.

SMALLWOOD: Old Scottish poem. Early eighth century.

RILTHE: I don't think I recall that one, Mr. Smallwood.

SMALLWOOD: Well, it's written in Old English. Religious verse with a little mythology sprinkled in for good flavor. One of the finest of its kind. A fragment of it is inscribed on a stone cross in Scotland. *(From his pocket, he produces a cylinder of breath mints.)* Care for a mint?

RILTHE: No, but thank you.

SMALLWOOD: *(Taking one, returning the rest)* Now in this poem the poet describes a dream. Lyrically. There's a kind of music to the words, so to speak. And in this dream, the Rood, or the *True Cross*, speaks to the poet in a friendly way like you or I might visit with someone after Sunday service. And in this friendly voice the Rood tells the story of its own history; how it came to be; how it had been willed into the world. The geometry of its creation, as it were. And the Rood urges him to promote its cult. Urges him to tip the buckets of devotion. To spill the passion, so to speak. And the poet does. He does the very thing.

RILTHE: And how is that?

SMALLWOOD: Well, he writes the poem.

RILTHE: I didn't know all that, Mister Smallwood.

SMALLWOOD: Listen, I will speak of the best of dreams, of what I dreamed at midnight when men and their wives were at rest. It seemed to me that I saw a most rare tree reach high aloft, wound in light, brightest of beams...

RILTHE: Is that the poem?

SMALLWOOD: It's just the beginning.

RILTHE: Well, I must say there's a lovely flow to it.

SMALLWOOD: It flows with the best of them...do you think you have an understanding of that kind of passion, Rilthe?

RILTHE: I do, Mister Smallwood. I believe I do.

SMALLWOOD: Well, that's good because you make a fine cross.

RILTHE: Well, thank you.

SMALLWOOD: A mighty fine one, indeed.

RILTHE: My children are fine workers.

SMALLWOOD: I'm sure they are. You and your husband must be proud.

RILTHE: We're all good bucket tippers here in the Klieg camp.

(*Awkward pause*)

SMALLWOOD: So...

RILTHE: So...

(*Everyone is still.* SMALLWOOD *smiles, looks over the crosses one final time.*)

SMALLWOOD: I think I'll take the whole lot of them.

RILTHE: Good Lord.

SMALLWOOD: The Lord is good indeed.

RILTHE: All of them?

SMALLWOOD: That's right, Rilthe.

RILTHE: Are you sure?

SMALLWOOD: I don't pass on a fine product when I see one.

(RILTHE *nods to* AMOS, *who places a hand on* AVIS *and* EPHESIA'*s shoulders.*)

AMOS, AVIS & EPHESIA: Thank you Mister Smallwood.

SMALLWOOD: Oh, you're quite welcome.

RILTHE: *(Containing excitement)* Amos, let's get these properly boxed. Avis you know where the filler is. Ephesia, entertain Mister Smallwood while I get the ledgers settled.

(RILTHE *exits.* AMOS *and* AVIS *exit.* SMALLWOOD *joins* EPHESIA *on the sofa.*)

SMALLWOOD: Well. That was easy. *(Wiping his brow)* Whew. Of all the years I've been making my procurements for the Church I have never seen ornaments the likes of those. Clean. Hard. Good weight to em. Thank you for the handsome flower. Ephesia: now there's a pretty name.

EPHESIA: Thanksgiving.

SMALLWOOD: Thanksgiving?

EPHESIA: That's how Mother prefers us to express gratitude.

SMALLWOOD: Spose it's better than sayin Easter or Christmas.

EPHESIA: When we're hungry we say "Deliver us Lord from the righteousness of our longing."

SMALLWOOD: Longing, huh?

EPHESIA: When we're angry we say "Deliver us Lord from our pride."

SMALLWOOD: Pride's a tricky one.

EPHESIA: And when we flush the toilet we say "Christ has died, Christ has risen, Christ will come again."

(SMALLWOOD *laughs.*)

SMALLWOOD: Yep. Good Old Ephesians. Body of Christ, temple of Christ, bride of Christ. Tenth book of the New Testament. There's power in the number ten.

EPHESIA: There's a hole in it.

SMALLWOOD: A hole?

EPHESIA: In the zero.

SMALLWOOD: Zero is a perfect number. It isn't broken or slanted in any way. It's endowed with sanctity.

EPHESIA: There's nothing inside of it.

SMALLWOOD: It has symmetry.

EPHESIA: It bores me.

SMALLWOOD: Well, now I wouldn't say all that.

EPHESIA: I would.

(SMALLWOOD *offers a stick of gum from his pocket.*)

SMALLWOOD: Chewing gum?

(She accepts it, puts it in her pocket.)

SMALLWOOD: Ephesians. Slides right in there between Galatians and Philippians. And Amos—now there's a Bible name, too. Earliest minor prophet. "Let justice roll down like waters, and righteousness like an ever-flowing stream." ...And then there's the young fella.

EPHESIA: Avis isn't in the Bible.

SMALLWOOD: No, I don't believe so.

EPHESIA: Chick's not in the Bible either.

SMALLWOOD: Chick?

EPHESIA: She lives in the attic.

SMALLWOOD: The attic.

EPHESIA: Yep. Behind a big steel door. There's a slot in it where we pass her her food.

(Awkward pause)

SMALLWOOD: I used to sell the bible. You believe that? King James Version. Perhaps the noblest monument of prose in the history of the English language. Lugged em around in a suitcase. Shoulder still locks up on me when it's humid.

EPHESIA: I don't like the bible.

SMALLWOOD: Some good lessons in that book.

EPHESIA: Too many old people.

SMALLWOOD: You don't like old people?

EPHESIA: They smell.

SMALLWOOD: Do you like young people?

EPHESIA: Too mean.

SMALLWOOD: Well, who do you like?

EPHESIA: I like pheasants.

SMALLWOOD: Pheasants?

EPHESIA: I had one once.

SMALLWOOD: Is that right?

EPHESIA: I found it in the meadow. It was walking like a person. Walked right up to me.

SMALLWOOD: Did you feed it?

EPHESIA: I put it in a box and brought it home.

SMALLWOOD: Does it still walk like a person?

EPHESIA: It's dead.

SMALLWOOD: Oh.

EPHESIA: Yep.

SMALLWOOD: Well, it must be awfully hard for a bird to adapt to the home.

EPHESIA: Amos killed it. He scorched it in the kiln.
When it started to burn it opened its beak and made
a face like it was thirsty.

(Awkward pause)

EPHESIA: And I like archery.

SMALLWOOD: Good sport.

EPHESIA: I'm a Sagittarius.

SMALLWOOD: Huh.

EPHESIA: I'm sociable and I like traveling, learning and
philosophy.

SMALLWOOD: Is that right?

EPHESIA: And with the right person I make a strong
domestic partner. That's what I'm going to be.

SMALLWOOD: A Sagittarius or a strong domestic
partner?

EPHESIA: An archer.

SMALLWOOD: Archery takes a steady hand.

EPHESIA: I'm gonna get a bow, start practicing. I want
to move to the mountains someday. Live in a log cabin.
Cook my own food. Plant a vegetable garden.

SMALLWOOD: Can be dangerous up there. And cold.

EPHESIA: I like danger.

SMALLWOOD: Wild animals.

EPHESIA: Animals are better than people

SMALLWOOD: Bear. Cougars. Mountain lions. Different
laws apply in the mountains. The elevation thins the
oxygen supply. Funny things happen up there.

EPHESIA: You think you know everything.

SMALLWOOD: Well, in all my years I'd say I've learned a thing or two about a thing or two, but I wouldn't claim omniscience.

EPHESIA: Whatever.

SMALLWOOD: Omniscience is when one posses authority of knowledge. A sort of universal insight into a great many things.

EPHESIA: Sounds like a retarded fish.

SMALLWOOD: A retarded fish?

EPHESIA: *(Mocking)* A retarded fish? ...You bore me, Lorenzo.

SMALLWOOD: I do?

EPHESIA: Now the rood, or *true cross*, speaks to the poet in a friendly way. Like you or I might visit with someone after Sunday service...

SMALLWOOD: Well, I'm glad you were paying attention.

EPHESIA: So boring.

SMALLWOOD: How old are you, Ephesia?

EPHESIA: Old enough.

SMALLWOOD: Old enough for what?

(EPHESIA *starts to whistle.*)

SMALLWOOD: You're not entertaining me very well.

EPHESIA: Well you can always pump your hand.

SMALLWOOD: Is that right?

EPHESIA: Yep.

SMALLWOOD: How does one pump one's hand?

EPHESIA: What did the wolf say to the chicken?

SMALLWOOD: Wolf?

EPHESIA: It's a riddle. What did the wolf say to the chicken?

SMALLWOOD: Well I don't know.

EPHESIA: He said what fine feathers you have.

SMALLWOOD: *(Playing along)* What fine feathers you have.

EPHESIA: And how does the chicken reply?

SMALLWOOD: I spose he'd say Thank you.

EPHESIA: *She*. The Chicken's a *she*.

SMALLWOOD: Then I spose *she'd* say Thank you.

EPHESIA: Nope. The chicken replies Thank you, Mister Wolf, would you like to see where I lay my eggs?

SMALLWOOD: Oh. Of course.

EPHESIA: Beep, beep, baby.

SMALLWOOD: Beep beep?

EPHESIA: Baby.

SMALLWOOD: Huh.

(Pause)

EPHESIA: You have to be able to control your heart.

SMALLWOOD: I don't think I follow you, Ephesia

EPHESIA: I'm back to archery.

SMALLWOOD: Well, I'm glad you're back.

EPHESIA: Heart control's very important.

SMALLWOOD: And how's that, Ephesia?

EPHESIA: You have to make it slow down, Lorenzo.

SMALLWOOD: I see.

EPHESIA: You have to count the beats.

SMALLWOOD: Well.

EPHESIA: Yep.

SMALLWOOD: There are many chambers to the heart.

(She rolls her eyes.)

SMALLWOOD: So tell me, Ephesia. How does one do that?

EPHESIA: Do what?

SMALLWOOD: Control one's heart?

EPHESIA: Breathing exercises.

(She takes a small paper sack out of her pocket and starts to suck the air from it very quickly, holds her breath. SMALLWOOD mimes drawing the string on a bow, aiming at EPHESIA. He releases the bow and mimes pulling on a string towards her. When he reaches her, he gently places his hands over her heart.)

SMALLWOOD: Bullseye

(RILTHE enters with a three part invoice. SMALLWOOD returns to his original position on the sofa.)

RILTHE: The boys should be up in a minute. They're just taping up some boxes.

(She hands the invoice to SMALLWOOD. He opens his briefcase, writes a check. AMOS and AVIS enter with two large boxes, start to pack the crosses.)

RILTHE: Ephesia, help your brothers.

(EPHESIA crosses to the display tables, helps AMOS and AVIS.)

SMALLWOOD: Sometimes I get a strong feeling when I start a new business relation, Rilthe. A premonition of sorts.

RILTHE: Intuition saved the turkey from many a hunter's rifle.

SMALLWOOD: The kind of hunch that glimmers like a very bright color.

RILTHE: Are you talking about a prophecy, Mister Smallwood?

SMALLWOOD: Now I'm not one to go round spinning auguries, Rilthe. It's a feeling that lives somewhere between your skin and your clothes.

RILTHE: Maybe it's your method of laundering.

(SMALLWOOD *laughs. The sound of a walker and footfalls descending the stairs cases can be heard.*)

SMALLWOOD: I have a hunch that you roods are going to vend like good pastries, Rilthe.

(RILTHE *quickly crosses to the coat rack.*)

RILTHE: Well, I hope they do, Mister Smallwood.

SMALLWOOD: Just expanded my territory, too. Couldn't be timelier.

(SMALLWOOD *hands the check to* RILTHE. *From the staircases the walker and footfalls grow louder.* RILTHE *quickly ushers* SMALLWOOD *toward the door.*)

RILTHE: Well, I look forward to your visits.

SMALLWOOD: And I look forward to calling on you. You have a fine family.

RILTHE: I'm sorry you missed my husband.

SMALLWOOD: I look forward to meeting him.

(RILTHE *shows him to the door.* AMOS *and* AVIS *enter from the basement and carry the packed boxes to the front door. The walker and footfalls are echoing at the foot of the stairs now.* RILTHE *practically shoves* SMALLWOOD *out the door.* SMALLWOOD *turns to* EPHESIA.)

SMALLWOOD: Just the loveliest light.

(He turns to RILTHE. *She hands him his hat and slicker.)*

SMALLWOOD: Good day, Rilthe.

RILTHE: Good day, Mister Smallwood. Have a safe trip.

(He exits. SLOAN *enters. He is mid-fifties, dressed in pajamas and a wrinkled housecoat. Socks without slippers. He is unshaved, his hair is a mess. He uses a walker and moves very slowly. He crosses to the dining room.)*

RILTHE: What are you doing, Sloan? ...Sloan?

(He stops. He looks around, confused.)

RILTHE: It's not time to eat yet, Sloan. You're not supposed to be down here.

SLOAN: I heard a voice. A man's voice. Like it was on the radio.

RILTHE: You're getting to be awfully unbridled with that walker.

SLOAN: You could feel the way everyone was listenin.

RILTHE: It was Mister Smallwood. He came to look at our crosses.

SLOAN: You can make a picture out of a voice. The arms. The legs. The hair. He was tall, ain't it?

RILTHE: He was rather tall, Sloan, yes.

SLOAN: Mailman come yet?

RILTHE: Yes he did, Sloan. Why, are you expecting something?

SLOAN: Good old U S mailman. Say hello, give him a wave. You can depend on that guy every time.

RILTHE: I'll make sure to greet him for you next time.

*(*SLOAN *starts to look under the table, behind the pews.)*

RILTHE: What are you looking for, Sloan?

SLOAN: My hat.

RILTHE: What hat?

SLOAN: Party hat.

RILTHE: You don't have a party hat, Sloan.

SLOAN: Made it outta paper.

RILTHE: You're confused, Sloan. You're confused and you need to rest.

SLOAN: I'm gonna wear it skatin.

RILTHE: There will be no skating, Sloan.

SLOAN: Shag's got my skate key. I gotta get my skate key.

RILTHE: You need to take your medicine, Sloan. You need to take your medicine and go back upstairs.

SLOAN: Hat. Skate key. For the parade.

RILTHE: What parade, Sloan?

SLOAN: Halloween parade. I'm goin as a ghost.

RILTHE: You fell, Sloan. You had an accident. It was raining and you slipped and hurt yourself. You're sick and you're going to get better.

(SLOAN *starts to shiver.*)

RILTHE: What's wrong?

SLOAN: Cold in here.

RILTHE: It's warm as a bakery in here.

SLOAN: Like it's gonna snow.

RILTHE: We won't see snow for two more months, Sloan.

SLOAN: The snow's smart. It knows when to come.

*(AMOS enters. RILTHE motions to him. He removes a bottle
of pills from his pocket, hands it to her.)*

RILTHE: Take your medicine, Sloan. Take your medicine
and go back to bed.

*(She hands him a pill and he takes it. AMOS and AVIS enter
from the front door. RILTHE motions to AMOS to escort
SLOAN back upstairs. AMOS takes his arm and they exit to
the stairwell.)*

SLOAN: *(To AMOS)* I'm goin as a ghost. I gotta get my
skate key.

(Lights fade.)

Scene Two

*(An hour later. RILTHE is sitting at the dining room table.
There is a towel wrapped around her shoulders. EPHESIA is
standing behind her, washing her hair, working up a thick
lather. RILTHE starts humming a church hymn.)*

RILTHE: We've had a good day, Daughter. A fine, fine,
day. A sign that better days are indeed ahead of us.
It'll keep those bankers off our porch. For a little while,
anyways.

EPHESIA: Avis wants to know if he can try out for the
basketball team.

RILTHE: He's too weak to play sports.

EPHESIA: He's been doing push-ups. He can do twenty.
I've seen him.

RILTHE: The ball is bigger than he is. He'll get crushed.

EPHESIA: He can spin the ball on his finger. He spins it
and taps it with his other hand so it keeps spinning.

RILTHE: I don't care if he can spin a Chevrolet and
change the transmission fluid.

EPHESIA: Tryouts are next Tuesday.

RILTHE: Well you tell him no.

EPHESIA: But they only last an hour.

RILTHE: Tell him no!

EPHESIA: Yes, ma'am.

RILTHE: A home is only as strong as its weakest wall, Daughter. Its most rusted pipe. A deficiency will run rampant if it isn't strengthened. Like a cancer floating in the blood stream. A wall cracks. A pipe bursts and causes flooding. We have to focus on our duties. Have a better understanding of the raw materials. A feel for the clay and an eye for the glaze.

EPHESIA: He said he would work extra at home.

RILTHE: That game is for the Negro. I have walked the streets where derelicts urinate into garbage cans of fire. I have seen the grime under their nails. The nicotine on their teeth. The sores on their mouths and their crooked fingers.

(AVIS *enters with a fresh basin of water. He takes the other basin and exits.* EPHESIA *starts to rinse* RILTHE's *hair.*)

RILTHE: There are shadows in the bone that spread during times of weakness. They settle in the spine and effect prostration and laziness. We do not dwell in that darkness. We do not know the smell of those afflicted genes. Our blood is thick with vitality. It is not thinned or tainted. Our teeth do not rot or fall out. Our tailbones do not protrude and welcome iniquity like the primates'.

(AVIS *enters and stands at the threshold of the dining room as if waiting for* RILTHE *to say something.*)

RILTHE: *(To* AVIS*)* Did you tell the Hobarts they could let their dog back out?

AVIS: No, ma'am.

RILTHE: Well, do your duty.

(AVIS *exits.* EPHESIA *continues to rinse* RILTHE's *hair.*
RILTHE *hums the church hymn.*)

(*Lights fade.*)

Scene Three

(*Same evening. It is very late. The basement.* EPHESIA *sits
Indian-style in front of the kiln, which emits an orange glow.
She wears a long night dress. There is a grocery bag beside
her. She removes the stick of gum* SMALLWOOD *had given
her. She unwraps it, considers it for a moment, and chews.
Then she takes out a small tube of lipstick, applies it clumsily
to her mouth.*)

(*In the living room,* AVIS *can be seen descending the
staircase, dressed in pajamas, carrying a grocery bag.
Just as he is about to head down to the basement,* CHICK
*appears in the living room. She wears a pillow case over her
head, a long lock of hair protruding from a slit. The light in
the living room is a strange, cerulean blue.* AVIS *sees* CHICK,
*freezes, stands very still. She silently beckons to him.
He remains frozen for a moment, then runs away.
Moments later he appears in the basement holding his
grocery bag. Ephesia and Avis stand in front of the kiln,
open its mouth, bend down and shout the following:*)

AVIS & EPHESIA: Chickenshit, fuckface, monkeydick,
vaginaballs, buttfuck on the window!

(*They close the kiln, gather around their grocery bags.*)

EPHESIA: Do you have the sheet?

AVIS: He found it.

EPHESIA: Who?

AVIS: Father.

EPHESIA: Did he flip your mattress?

AVIS: Nu-uh.

EPHESIA: Did he salt it?

AVIS: He didn't even carp me. I couldn't believe it. He said he needed the sheet for the parade.

EPHESIA: Something happened to him when he fell and hit his head, Avis. He walks around with his mouth hanging open.

AVIS: He's trying to breathe.

EPHESIA: How do you know?

AVIS: Cause he told me. He said he forgets.

EPHESIA: He forgets how to breathe?

AVIS: Uh-huh.

(Pause)

EPHESIA: What did you bring?

(AVIS removes a poster from the bag. He unrolls it. It's a poster of a black basketball player flying through the air. AVIS touches the legs. After a moment, EPHESIA takes the poster, crumples it, opens the door to the kiln.)

EPHESIA: Good-bye forever.

AVIS: Good-bye forever.

(She throws it in the kiln, closes the door.)

EPHESIA: What else?

(AVIS reaches into the bag and removes the hat he had found collecting garbage. He puts it on his head. It is too large and is tilted. EPHESIA corrects it. They play for a moment, then she takes the hat, crosses to the kiln, opens it.)

EPHESIA: Good-bye forever.

AVIS: Good-bye forever.

(She throws it in the kiln, closes the door.)

EPHESIA: What else?

(AVIS pulls out a pair of sneakers with platform toes.)

EPHESIA: What are those?

AVIS: Jumping shoes. *(He puts them on, jumps a few times.)* They make you jump higher.

EPHESIA: Can I try?

(AVIS takes them off. She puts them on and jumps very quietly. She stops and takes them off. She opens the door to the kiln. AVIS grabs the shoes from her.)

EPHESIA: Avis, you know the rules.

AVIS: What did you bring?

(From her bag she removes a pair of jeans. She slips them on under her night dress. She pulls the night dress up and starts to walk around, sashaying and teasing invisible construction workers. AVIS laughs. They sit quietly.)

AVIS: I heard her again.

EPHESIA: Chick?

AVIS: She was cryin.

EPHESIA: I think something bad's gonna happen to her, Avis. I hear Mother and Amos talking. I can't make out the words but I can feel it in their voices.

AVIS: Amos told me she wants to eat me.

EPHESIA: Avis, Chick's not gonna eat you!

AVIS: Amos says she's part goat part gorilla.

EPHESIA: He's just trying to scare you. Chick is totally human.

AVIS: How do you know?

EPHESIA: I've seen her.

AVIS: You have?

EPHESIA: I've been sneaking her books.

AVIS: She can *read*?

EPHESIA: I taught her.

AVIS: *What?!*

EPHESIA: I did. She's a total genius. She learned to read in like three weeks. I've been sneaking her books from my History class.

AVIS: What kind of books?

EPHESIA: Books about the Holocaust.

AVIS: You're sneaking her *Jewbooks*?!

EPHESIA: Don't say that, Avis. You sound like Amos. They're books about how the Jews had to hide during the war. It's no big deal. And she paints too.

AVIS: She paints *Jews*?

EPHESIA: No, she paints murals.

AVIS: What kind of murals?

EPHESIA: I don't know. I can't see because she stands in front of the slot. I steal stuff from art class. Brushes and tubes of paint. All sorts of colors. I sneak them to her.

AVIS: She's gonna eat you.

EPHESIA: That's crazy!

AVIS: She's gonna pull you through the slot.

(*The basement door suddenly opens and closes. The sound of descending footfalls.* EPHESIA *directs* AVIS *to hide. He quickly runs toward the shadows.* EPHESIA *frantically removes her jeans, opens the kiln, throws them in.*)

(*From the shadows we hear* AMOS' *voice.*)

AMOS: What did the wolf say to the chicken?

(EPHESIA *retreats.*)

AMOS: What did the wolf say to the chicken!

EPHESIA: What fine feathers you have.

AMOS: And how does the chicken reply?

EPHESIA: Thank you.

AMOS: How does the chicken reply!

EPHESIA: Thank you Mister Wolf...

(AMOS *can be seen now. He is bare-chested and there are pheasant feathers arranged in his hair. His is also holding what appears to be a long black wig. The wig has a barrette in it.*)

AMOS: Do it.

EPHESIA: ThankyouMisterWolfwouldyouliketoseewhere Ilaymyeggs?

(AMOS *removes the wooden pin from his belt loop.*)

AMOS: Take em down.

(*She hesitates.*)

AMOS: Go on.

(*She takes her pants down. He moves behind her, sets the black wig on her head very carefully, then removes a pheasant feather, strokes her arm with it. Then beckons her to the shadows.* EPHESIA *slowly follows him.*)

AMOS: Beep like the chicken.

EPHESIA: Beep...

AMOS: Beep like the chicken.

EPHESIA: Beep... beep.

AMOS: Beep like the chicken!

EPHESIA: Beep beep.

(They disappear into the shadows.)

Scene Four

(There is a large statue in the center of the dining room. It is covered in brown paper and bound with string. There is a folding chair at the head of the table. There is a white sheet folded neatly at the edge of the table. RILTHE enters with the black medical bag. She places the bag on the table next to the folded sheet. Moments later, AMOS enters from the staircase. His clothes are soaked and he is limping. He is drying himself with a towel.)

RILTHE: Well?

AMOS: He kicked me.

RILTHE: He kicked you?

AMOS: Wouldn't let me shave him. I got halfway and he starts goin crazy.

RILTHE: Didn't you tell him he could use the Aqua Velva?

AMOS: He tried to drink it.

RILTHE: Lord. Is he showered?

AMOS: He wouldn't stand up so I drew him a bath.

RILTHE: You look like you joined him.

AMOS: Well, that's because he splashed me every damn time I came near him with the soapstone.

RILTHE: Dear God.

AMOS: And he kept screamin for John Jimmy Tom.

RILTHE: John Jimmy Tim?! Who on earth is that?!

AMOS: He said it was his friend the dancing water turkey.

RILTHE: Dancing water turkey?!

AMOS: That's what he said.

RILTHE: Of all the lunacy.

AMOS: Kept asking for his party hat, too.

RILTHE: Did you tell him it would've been ruined?

AMOS: I told him.

RILTHE: What about his blue suit?

AMOS: He wouldn't put it on.

RILTHE: Why not?

AMOS: He kept sayin there was a ghostwizard in it.

RILTHE: Ghostwizard?!

AMOS: That's what he said.

RILTHE: That man hasn't used a sentence with sense in it for I don't know how long.

AMOS: Every time I brought it near him he started cryin.

RILTHE: But that's the suit I made for him when we were married. He used to wear it to church every Sunday.

AMOS: He said if he put it on the ghostwizard would turn his heart to stone.

RILTHE: If the Good Lord intended healing to be such a riddle we'd live in a world full of half-wits and pinheads.

AMOS: He fouled himself again, too.

RILTHE: Oh for the love of Job.

AMOS: And he was smilin like he knew what he was doin.

RILTHE: Well of course he knew what he was doing! He's not a quadripelegic! ...Did any get on the floor?

AMOS: No ma'am, I caught most of it.

RILTHE: To think that this is the same man who I slept beside and made congress with for thirty years. The man who built my factory with his bare hands and taught us the magic of the kiln. The man who could hold his hand over a flame longer than most people can look at one. To think that this is the same man who worked harder than a pack mule and came home to manage our factory and teach the scriptures to his children. To think that this is the same man who once fought in a war on a dark continent and brought home medals and ribbons and a glorious necklace of the ears of the mongrels he'd exterminated. To think that this is the same man. It's like an awful joke, Amos. An awful, horrible joke.

AMOS: He put his dress greens on.

RILTHE: He put his dress greens on?

(SLOAN *enters from the stairwell with his walker. He is wearing his dress greens over a T-shirt. The jacket is unbuttoned. He isn't wearing shoes. His face is half-shaven and his hair is overly combed. He slowly crosses to the table, stops and stares at the statue.*)

SLOAN: There's a dead guy in the house.

RILTHE: It's a statue.

SLOAN: Better call the fire department.

RILTHE: It's a statue of a Saint.

SLOAN: Either them or the morgue. Looks like it's already wrapped up and ready to go.

RILTHE: Look at me, Sloan.

(*He turns to her.*)

RILTHE: That is a statue of Saint Anthony. We're going to set it on the porch.

SLOAN: I had a porch once. Weatherproofed it with a paintbrush. Homers Formby. Good old Homers Formby.

RILTHE: Yes, I know you had a porch, Sloan. You still do. And we're going to set the statue of Saint Anthony on it. Saint Anthony is the patron saint of the depraved and missing. He's going to help us find you again. It's a decoration.

SLOAN: I had a decoration once. Pocket watch. I had a train on the back of it. Kept it in my pocket. It would tell you the time right up to the second. Kept atomic time. Right up to the second.

RILTHE: Sloan, why did you kick Amos?

SLOAN: He wouldn't give me my hat.

RILTHE: Amos, give him his hat.

(AMOS *produces a triangular hat made out of newspapers, hands it to* SLOAN, *exits.*)

RILTHE: You look very nice, Sloan.

(RILTHE *motions at* AMOS *to leave.* AMOS *sets* SLOAN's *walker near him, exits.*)

SLOAN: Mailman come yet?

RILTHE: Yes, he did, Sloan. He came.

SLOAN: Did he say Hello?

RILTHE: He said Hello.

SLOAN: Did he give a wave?

RILTHE: Yes, he did. He gave a wave and I told him hello for you.

SLOAN: Good old U S mailman.

RILTHE: Sloan, why wouldn't you put your blue suit on?

SLOAN: Ghostwizard.

RILTHE: That's nonsense.

SLOAN: He was wearin it.

RILTHE: That's crazy, Sloan. Those are crazy rickety thoughts and you aren't to think them. There's no such thing as a ghostwizard. And it's *Grand Wizard*, Sloan. *Grand Wizard.*

SLOAN: Let the fire fly through the night...

RILTHE: That's right, Sloan. Let the fire fly through the night, as the rain will purify the light.

(She wipes shaving cream off his face.)

RILTHE: Do you know why I called you down here, Sloan?

SLOAN: Cause it's gonna snow.

RILTHE: No, Sloan, that's not why I called you down here.

SLOAN: It's gonna snow and everything's gonna get covered.

RILTHE: Yes, Sloan, eventually it will snow. When winter comes. And the streets will be white and the trees will be white and everything will look clean and good.

SLOAN: You want me to disappear in it.

RILTHE: That will never happen, Sloan. That's ridiculous. You are going to get better and things will be just like they were before.

SLOAN: And the stairs don't feel the same. Somethin happened to the stairs.

RILTHE: Nothing's happened to the stairs.

SLOAN: Someone keeps changin em.

RILTHE: *(Taking his hand)* Just settle down now, Sloan.
No one's changing anything. Just relax. *(Fixing his hair)*
Sloan, do you remember what we started to talk about
before you got sick? About Chick?

SLOAN: I hear her sometimes.

RILTHE: I know Sloan. We all hear her.

SLOAN: She sounds real upset.

RILTHE: Do you remember how we talked about how
sad she is and how were going to help her?

SLOAN: Sounds like she's floatin away.

RILTHE: That's because she's sad, Sloan. That's because
she's so very sad... Sloan, since your accident we
haven't been as financially stable as we have been in
the past.

SLOAN: I worked in a stable once. Fed horses in a stable.

RILTHE: I know, Sloan. You did. When you were a boy
you worked in a stable that's correct. But that's not
what I'm talking about right now.

SLOAN: There was this black one named Jackie
Robinson. Blackest horse you'll ever see. Good old
Jackie Robinson. Whinny whinny.

RILTHE: Sloan, since your accident, we've been getting
a disability check instead of your normal salary. And
although it helps, it's not the same. Even with your
veterans pension it's not the same. Not nearly the same.
And now the bank is threatening us. Because things
are slight. Despite the good week we had when Mister
Smallwood came, things are still slight. It's like the
three bears. Do you remember the story I read to you
the other day about the three bears?

(He nods.)

RILTHE: Well, Sloan, it's like the three bears eating three bowls of porridge every day. And then one day the porridge starts to run out and they only get two bowls. And it's very hard to feed three hungry bears with two bowls of porridge. Do you understand me, Sloan?

SLOAN: I saw a bear eat a phonebook once.

RILTHE: I'm not talking about the Yellow Pages, Sloan! I'm talking about economics and foreclosure! About bankers and their little adding machines. About the harsh reality of money, Sloan!

SLOAN: Well, I got money.

RILTHE: You do?

SLOAN: Sure. I been savin it.

RILTHE: For how long, Sloan?

SLOAN: Oh, a long time. Bout forty years.

RILTHE: Well, where on God's earth is it?

SLOAN: I got it hid

RILTHE: Well would you mind sharing it with me?

SLOAN: Sure.

(SLOAN *reaches into his pocket and removes an old felt pouch. He hands it to* RILTHE. *She opens it. A few small coins fall out.* SLOAN *starts to arrange them on the table.*)

RILTHE: There's thirty-nine cents here, Sloan.

SLOAN: I found this one here under the water heater. And if you breathe on this one and wipe it with a cloth it shines. And this one here's got a face on it that sort of looks like you. Either you or George Washingmachine. I put that one in a special place. Real close to me.

(RILTHE *gathers the coins, re-pouches them, and hands them back to* SLOAN.)

RILTHE: Sloan, before your accident we talked about helping Chick. About helping her sleep.

SLOAN: Them bears don't need no help sleeping.

RILTHE: But the bears aren't sad, Sloan. And Chick is so very sad and there's not enough porridge. Chick wants to sleep, Sloan. It's time to help her sleep. *(She removes a hypodermic needle from the bag.)* I want you to go upstairs with Amos, Sloan. I want you to go upstairs and give this to Chick. Just like we talked bout before. Amos is going to show you how to do it.

(She places the hypo back in the bag and pushes it toward him. He stares at it.)

SLOAN: I get pictures of her in my head. At night.

RILTHE: Dreams, Sloan. They're called dreams.

SLOAN: Had one last night. Her face wasn't big no more. It was small. And she had regular parts on it. Regular teeth. Regular nose. Regular eyes. She was singin. But her voice wasn't words. It was the wind. Started blowin all over the place. And she gave me a flower. It was big as a tree. Thousands of colors. Millions of em. Blues and purples and golds. Colors that ain't even invented yet. And the wind in her voice was blowin through the colors. I could feel it inside me. Warmest thing I ever felt in my life. She told me it was a monkey flower. A monkey flower from the top of the mountain. That's what she told me. I'm gonna find me one of them.

(SLOAN slowly exits back up the stairs with his walker, leaving the black medical bag on the table. AMOS appears from the kitchen. He and RILTHE stare at each other. EPHESIA enters, dressed in a plaid Catholic school uniform. Her arms are full of books. There is an arrangement of freshly picked wild asters on top of her books, a far-off look on her face.)

RILTHE: Where's your brother?

EPHESIA: I don't know.

RILTHE: Wasn't he on the bus?

EPHESIA: No ma'am.

RILTHE: Why do you have so many books? Every time you come home your arms are full of books any more.

EPHESIA: Extra credit.

RILTHE: Well, aren't you the ambitious one. Little Miss Enterpriser. *(She grabs the folded sheet stands, and lets the bottom fall to the floor. There is a large blood stain down the center of it.)* And if there are certain questions you need to ask me about the female anatomy, you may pose them now.

EPHESIA: I know about it.

RILTHE: Well then you'd better start applying your wisdom. This is the fourth day in a row I've found your linens soiled like this. If you need stronger gauzings I will provide them. *(She removes an enormous maxi pad from her apron, takes the flowers, and places it on top of the stack of books.)* There is no room for shame or embarrassment in these matters, Daughter. If God intended the fertility of our loins to spill about in the streets he would have made us goats or cattle and birthed us in a pasture.

EPHESIA: Yes ma'am.

RILTHE: Now go change and get to work. Mister Smallwood is coming tomorrow and your tables need polishing. *(She exits.)*

RILTHE: *(To* AMOS*)* Go find your brother.

(Lights fade as RILTHE *sits holding the sheet.)*

Scene Five

(Two hours later. AVIS stands on top of a chair in the center of the dining room, in front of the statue. RILTHE sits beside him embroidering, a basketball at her feet. AMOS stands behind her with his clipboard, the wooden pin in his belt loop. EPHESIA is in the living room polishing the surfaces of the wooden display tables. AVIS stands very still and looks straight ahead. He is wearing his Catholic school uniform. His shirt is damp with sweat.)

RILTHE: Do you love me, Avis?

AVIS: Yes ma'am.

RILTHE: Do you love this family?

AVIS: Yes, ma'am.

RILTHE: Do you love your church?

AVIS: Yes, ma'am.

RILTHE: Do you love your God?

AVIS: Yes, ma'am.

RILTHE: Old Testament.

AVIS: Genesis, Exodus, Leviticus, Numbers, Deuteronomy, Joshua, Judges, Ruth, First and Second Samuel, first and second Kings, First and second Chronicles, Ezra-

RILTHE: Faster!

AVIS: Nehemiah Esther Job Psalms Proverbs Ecclesiastes Song of Solomon Isaiah Jeremiah Lamentations Ezekiel Daniel Hosea Joel—

RILTHE: Faster!

AVIS: AmosObadiahJonahMicahNahumHabakkuk Zephaniah HaggaiZechaiahMalachi.

RILTHE: Arms out.

(He spreads his arms out wide.)

RILTHE: Step.

(He steps down and then back up to the seat of the chair.)

AVIS: Romans four-five but to him that worketh not but believeth on him that justifieth the ungodly his faith is counted as righteousness.

RILTHE: Stand.

(He steps back to the seat of the chair.)

RILTHE: Arms down.

(AVIS lets his arms drop to his sides. AMOS stands before him. He removes the wooden pin from his belt loop. He holds it firmly. RILTHE continues her embroidery.)

AMOS: New Testament.

AVIS: Matthew, Mark, Luke, John, Acts Romans, First and Second Corinthians, Galatians, Ephesians, Philippians, Colossians, First and Second Thessalonians, First and Second Timothy—

AMOS: Faster!

AVIS: TitusPhilemonHebrewsJames—

AMOS: Faster!

AVIS: FirstandSecondPeterFirstSecondandThirdJohnJude Revelation.

AMOS: Arms out.

(AVIS spreads his arms. AMOS places a stack of composition tablets on ether hand. Corrects his posture a bit, using the wooden pin.)

AMOS: Step.

(AVIS repeats the stepping exercise.)

AVIS: Romans four-five but to him that worketh not but believeth on him that justifieth the ungodly his faith is counted as righteousness.

(He continues stepping. AMOS waits until AVIS is genuinely exhausted.)

AMOS: Stand.

(AVIS stands on the chair with his arms still stretched. AMOS takes the tablets off his hands. They tremble visibly.)

AMOS: Arms down.

(AVIS lets his arms drop. RILTHE continues her embroidery.)

RILTHE: Do you love me, Avis?

AVIS: Yes ma'am.

RILTHE: Do you love this family?

AVIS: Yes, ma'am.

RILTHE: Do you love your Church?

AVIS: Yes, ma'am.

RILTHE: Do you love your God?

AVIS: Yes, ma'am.

RILTHE: If I find out that you're playing basketball in the park again I'll carp you so many times you won't recognize the sound of your own voice calling out, is that clear?

AVIS: Yes, ma'am.

RILTHE: Mister Smallwood is scheduled to arrive tomorrow morning and there's work to be done. Your duties are paramount. There is no time for games in the alleyway.

AVIS: Yes, ma'am.

(RILTHE hands the basketball to AMOS.)

RILTHE: Break it.

(AMOS *slides the wooden pin back into his belt loop, removes the utility knife from his snap pouch, punctures the ball.*)

RILTHE:*(To* AVIS*)* Now go sanitize yourself and help your sister.

(AVIS *dismounts from the chair and exits very slowly up the stairs.* AMOS *turns and stares at* EPHESIA. *She continues to polish a cross. He walks over to her and drops the punctured ball on one of the display tables. Lights fade as* RILTHE *continues her embroidery.*)

END OF ACT ONE

ACT TWO

Scene One

(The next morning. Sunlight pours through the stained glass window. A plate of plain doughnuts has been set on the table. The wild asters are centered on the table. The display tables are set up at the threshold of the living room. Ceramic crosses are once again displayed. These crosses are longer and more intricate, perhaps more Gothic-looking. The statue of Saint Anthony has been move to the porch. A slow choir hymn plays from the phonograph. There is a knock at the door. RILTHE enters room the kitchen, quickly adjust the flowers, primps her hair, and moves to the door. She opens the door to SMALLWOOD. He is once again wearing the slicker and carrying the briefcase.)

SMALLWOOD: Morning, Rilthe.

RILTHE: Good morning, Mister Smallwood. Please come in.

(He enters. She takes his slicker, hangs it on the coat rack.)

RILTHE: Please help yourself to doughnuts.

SMALLWOOD: I will, thank you. *(He crosses to the table, takes a doughnut.)*

RILTHE: How was your trip?

SMALLWOOD: I'll tell you, Rilthe, there's nothing like an October sun to edify the autumn landscape.

RILTHE: Oh, the leaves are heavenly this year.

SMALLWOOD: So many shades you have to consult a catalog of color just to name them.

RILTHE: The trees over by Saint Michael's are just mighty.

SMALLWOOD: Saw a stand of poplars in Plano that gave the color gold a new meaning.

RILTHE: It's my favorite season.

SMALLWOOD: Mine too, Rilthe. Mine too...I see you have yourself a permanent suitor on the porch.

RILTHE: Excuse me?

SMALLWOOD: Saint Anthony.

RILTHE: Oh, of course.

SMALLWOOD: Thought it was your husband fixing the mailbox at first.

RILTHE: Is it daunting?

SMALLWOOD: Oh no, not at all. Just man-like. So very man-like. Good old Anthony. The great Detective Saint with the Italian name. Finder of things lost.

RILTHE: We were lucky enough to take it off the hands of Saint Patrick's.

SMALLWOOD: Is that right?

RILTHE: It was just taking up space in their grotto.

SMALLWOOD: That's where I've seen it—right next to the blue stone of Mary. It made the loveliest ensemble.

RILTHE: The children from the neighborhood were violating it with slingshots and bee bee guns.

SMALLWOOD: Isn't that a shame.

RILTHE: Children and their wicked toys.

SMALLWOOD: The seed of the pagan tree will germinate and sow a deviant timber.

RILTHE: Nursed from the froth of the mud puddle, these hooligans.

SMALLWOOD: It's a sad state of affairs.

RILTHE: So I talked with Father Gentry and made a small donation and Sloan and I had the imperfections restored.

SMALLWOOD: What a nice thing to do.

RILTHE: We thought it would freshen up the neighborhood.

SMALLWOOD: Well good for you, Rilthe. I'm sure God is watching through his crystal spyglass.

(AVIS enters with a cup of coffee and a saucer, gives it to SMALLWOOD, offers his hand. SMALLWOOD greets AVIS with a handshake.)

SMALLWOOD: Now there's a firm one. How are you, Avis?

AVIS: Fine, thanksgiving.

(AVIS crosses to a spot near RILTHE, stands very still with his arms behind his back. EPHESIA enters with a boutonniere, hands it to SMALLWOOD.)

SMALLWOOD: The Lord created fine daughters and capable sons for a good reason. Hello Ephesia.

EPHESIA: Hi, Mister Smallwood.

(She crosses to AVIS, stands very still with her hands behind her back.)

SMALLWOOD: And I believe that leaves one child more to greet.

RILTHE: Oh, Amos is out on the coal run. With this batch I'm afraid we've exhausted our kiln fuel.

SMALLWOOD: Fine work requires a hardy energy source.

(Once again, a loud moaning can be heard.)

SMALLWOOD: Those darn floorboards.

RILTHE: Old wood and tricky weather.

SMALLWOOD: Nothing like a house with a little personality.

(The moaning continues for a moment and then ceases.)

SMALLWOOD: Well, then. Shall we?

(He takes his saucer and coffee to the living room where AVIS and EPHESIA are seated on the sofa. RILTHE follows. He studies the new crosses.)

SMALLWOOD: Rilthe, I must say you have done it again.

RILTHE: We've attenuated the vertical staff a bit.

SMALLWOOD: Striking, striking work.

RILTHE: This batch may work higher on the wall.

SMALLWOOD: I think it does. Clock height, at least. And the glaze...

RILTHE: We thinned it a bit this time. We thought it appropriate for its larger size.

SMALLWOOD: Don't want to blind em into the parking lots.

RILTHE: They're a little more angular.

(SMALLWOOD studies the crosses.)

RILTHE: Would you care for another doughnut?

SMALLWOOD: No, thank you. Let's just get these boxed up. The sooner I get them distributed the sooner they can touch others.

RILTHE: Avis, let's get these boxed.

(AVIS exits.)

RILTHE: *(Exiting)* Ephesia, entertain Mister Smallwood while I settle other matters.

(EPHESIA crosses to the sofa, sits. SMALLWOOD joins her on the sofa.)

SMALLWOOD: So... Double so... Double so with a Chiclet on top... Acquire any pheasants lately? Saw one just the other day over by my shoe barber's. Hoppin through the storm grass. Hoppin just like a person.

(He offers a piece of candy from his pocket. She doesn't accept it.)

SMALLWOOD: How did the chicken cross the firmament?

(She shrugs her shoulders.)

SMALLWOOD: Like this.

(He looks up at the sky and mimes the sign of the cross. He laughs. He sighs. She is silent.)

SMALLWOOD: *(Singing)*
I had a dog and his name was Blue
I had a dog and his name was Blue
I had a dog and his name was Blue
Betcha five dollars he's a good dog too...

Singing here Blue
You're a good dog...

Beep beep.

(She doesn't respond.)

SMALLWOOD: I brought you a gift.

(He opens his briefcase and removes a child's bow, produces a pheasant feather, arranged it in his hair, hands her the bow.)

SMALLWOOD: Thought you could get a jump start on the competition. Throw a coupla targets on a tree or a post or somethin. From what I hear, you, use these three fingers and hold the arrow with these two

(Fanning his fingers, pointing to the space between his index and middle fingers) Keep her steady on the draw and let her rip. Maybe next time I'll bring you some arrows.

(RILTHE enters from the kitchen. EPHESIA quickly hides her gift under the sofa. SMALLWOOD removes the pheasant feather. RILTHE smiles at SMALLWOOD and exits into her bedroom.)

SMALLWOOD: How are your breathing exercises coming along?

(EPHESIA reaches under apron and down her pants and smears blood on the front of her apron. She attempts to spell out "HELP". It turns out very crudely. She starts to silently cry and tremble.)

SMALLWOOD: Oh child, what has happened?

(RILTHE enters from her bedroom holding a vinyl record album. EPHESIA conceals the bloody section of her apron.)

RILTHE: Ephesia, go help your brother.

(EPHESIA exits. RILTHE hands SMALLWOOD an invoice. He takes out his checkbook and starts to write a check. They exchange check and invoice.)

RILTHE: Mister Smallwood, I thought you might like to have this.

(She proffers the record album. He accepts it.)

RILTHE: It's the Shambly Hopelight Choir. Their Christmas revue.

SMALLWOOD: Why thank you, Rilthe. What a lovely thought.

(SLOAN enters from the stairs carrying a shovel. He is without the walker, dressed in his pajamas and housecoat. He also wears his paper hat.)

RILTHE: What on God's earth are you doing with that shovel, Sloan?

SLOAN: I was gonna put him in the ground.

RILTHE: Put who in the ground?

SLOAN: The dead guy.

RILTHE: *(Seizing the shovel)* I told you before, Sloan, Saint Anthony is a statue and we set him on the front porch.

SLOAN: *(To* SMALLWOOD*)* You ain't the dead guy are you?

SMALLWOOD: No, I'm afraid I'm not.

RILTHE: Mister Smallwood, this is my husband, Sloan.

SMALLWOOD: *(Extending his hand)* How do you do, Mr. Klieg?

*(*SLOAN *stares at his hand.)*

RILTHE: Sloan recently had an accident, Mister Smallwood.

SLOAN: *(To* SMALLWOOD*)* When you're falling you're not supposed to use your hands.

*(*SMALLWOOD *retracts his hand.)*

RILTHE: His name is Mister Smallwood, Sloan. He's the gentlemen who's been placing our crosses.

SLOAN: You're the radio guy. You're tall because your voice is tall.

RILTHE: Where's your walker, Sloan?

SLOAN: *(To* SMALLWOOD*)* I used to walk on my hands. When I was a boy. Walked all over town. Right alongside the ice cream truck. Me and Funny Bob the Beagle. Good old Funny Bob.

SMALLWOOD: Sounds like fun, Mister Klieg.

SLOAN: Got some vanilla.

RILTHE: I suggest you go back upstairs and tend to you walker Sloan.

SLOAN: I made it fly.

RILTHE: You did not.

SLOAN: I made it fly after I captured Amos. I turned into a butterfly and blended right in. Right in with all the other can't-see-ems.

RILTHE: What on earth are you talking about?

SLOAN: The can't-see-ems and the not-supposed-to-knows.

(AVIS *and* EPHESIA *enter with boxes.*)

SMALLWOOD: Well, I think I should be heading back.

RILTHE: Oh, Mister Smallwood, I was just going to ask you if you'd like to join us for supper.

SMALLWOOD: Oh, no thank you. I have another appointment in Oswego. Gotta make good time.

SLOAN: I had a radio that had a voice just like yours. A M/F M. Copper dials. Wicker speaker screens. Mahogany arch. Best radio in the neighborhood.

SMALLWOOD: I'm sure it was, Mister Klieg.

RILTHE: I make a fine rack of lamb, Mister Smallwood. Lamb like you've never tasted before .

SMALLWOOD: No thank you, Rilthe, I'd better be getting on. I enjoyed visiting with you all today. It was nice to finally meet you, Mister Klieg. (*He crosses to the coat rack, grabs his slicker.*)

RILTHE: Good-bye, Mister Smallwood. Have a safe trip.

(*He exits.* AVIS *and* EPHESIA *follow with the boxes.* RILTHE *turns to* SLOAN, *aggravated.*)

SLOAN: Mailman come?

RILTHE: Yes, Sloan, the mailman came and he waved hello and I greeted him on your behalf!

SLOAN: Good old U S mailman.

RILTHE: You should be ashamed of yourself! Shame on you! Shame! Shame!

(AMOS *appears at the foot of the stairs. He is holding several pieces of rope that have been severed by his knife. He is very angry.*)

RILTHE: And you should be ashamed of yourself, too!

(SLOAN *turns and crosses to the stairs.*)

RILTHE: Make sure he takes his medication.

(AMOS *takes his arm and they exit up the stairs.* AVIS *enters from the front door carrying* SLOAN'*s walker, which is slightly bent from landing in the front yard.*)

RILTHE: (*To* AVIS) Take that up to your father.

(AVIS *exits up the stairs with the walker.*)

(*Lights fade.*)

Scene Two

(*Very late that evening. The living room. The light is a strange, cerulean blue.* AVIS *can be seen descending the staircase, dressed in pajamas, wearing his jumping shoes.* CHICK *appears in the living room, as she had at the end of* ACT ONE. *Once again, she wears a pillow case over her head.* AVIS *sees* CHICK, *freezes, stands very still. As before, she moves toward him. He remains frozen.* CHICK *slowly raises her hand as if to say hello.* AVIS *waves to her very quickly, and then exits down to the basement.* CHICK *disappears into the shadows.*)

(*In the basement,* AVIS *crosses to the basement, sits in front of kiln, waits. From off,* EPHESIA'*s voice can be heard.*)

EPHESIA: Chickenshit.

AVIS: Chickenshit fuckface.

EPHESIA: Chickenshit fuckface monkeydick.

AVIS: Chickenshit fuckface mokeydick vaginaballs.

(EPHESIA *appears in the basement, wearing her nightgown.*)

EPHESIA: Chickenshit fuckface monkeydick vaginaballs
buttfuck on the window.

AVIS & EPHESIA: Chickenshit fuckface monkeydick
vaginaballs buttfuck on the window.

(They sit.)

AVIS: I made the team. At practice you get to forget who
you are. It's like leaving your body. Running and
jumping. Offense, defense. Three-on-two, two-on-one
fast breaks. Two-two-one full court press.
One-three-one zone trap. Stair laps. Free-throw ladders.
Seagull slides. Suicide sprints. Mississippi tip drill.
When you play defense you keep your middle tight
like there's a fist in your stomach. You have to slide
your feet without crossing yours legs. If you cross your
legs you get beat. I can dribble through the whole team.
They think I'm going one way but then I'm not there.
I make myself smaller and they can't find me. I got
hops, too.

EPHESIA: What are hops?

AVIS: I can jump.

EPHESIA: Have you made any friends?

AVIS: His name is Sample. He's black.

EPHESIA:*(Excited) How* black?

AVIS: Black like a horse.

EPHESIA: What kind of a horse?

AVIS: Racehorse. And his hair's like wool.

EPHESIA: Like a rug?

AVIS: Like a sweater.

EPHESIA: What else?

AVIS: He's a forward and I'm a guard. Sometimes he plays guard-forward or forward-guard. When he jumps, the parts in his legs look like vegetables. And he smells different.

EPHESIA: Like what?

AVIS: Like bowling shoes... And he calls me G.

EPHESIA: G?

AVIS: Like What's up, G? He calls me G and I call him B. He says, What's up, G? And I go, What's up, B? And he puts money in his ears.

EPHESIA: Money?

AVIS: Nickels.

EPHESIA: In his ears?

(AVIS *produces two nickels, inserts them into both ears. He shows* EPHESIA *and then produces two more nickels, inserts nickels into her ears. They laugh and touch the nickels.*)

EPHESIA: What else?

AVIS: It's different.

EPHESIA: What's different?

AVIS: His thing.

EPHESIA: His pecker?

(AVIS *nods.*)

EPHESIA: How do you know?

AVIS: He showed it to me. In his basement. Behind the water heater. It doesn't have a knob on the end. The skin keeps going. Like an elephant trunk... I showed him mine, too.

EPHESIA: You did?

(AVIS *nods.*)

EPHESIA: What happened?

AVIS: He put his fingers out. Like this. And he touched it. My stomach died. His palm was white. Like there's a ghost in his hand. It felt like falling out of a tree. I'm a guard. He's a forward. I dribble the ball up court. I set it up for him. Down screen. Cross screen. Pick and roll. U C L A cut. Fake high pass low. Look away. But see it in your head. With the eyes in your head. I get him the ball. Bounce pass with a little English. He scores. And he looks at me. With his heart. I can feel it. No one's ever looked at me like that. He told me he wants to marry me. He said, 'I wanna marry you, G.' We don't kiss or anything. But we love each other. First game's Friday.

(EPHESIA *reaches under her nightgown and shows him the blood on her hand.*)

EPHESIA: It won't stop bleeding.

AVIS: What's it from?

EPHESIA: Amos.

(SLOAN *enters wearing his paper hat, dressed in his pajamas and housecoat. He is not using his walker. A pair of skates is slung over one shoulder. He is carrying a small paper sack. They are afraid. After a moment,* SLOAN *removes his paper hat and hands it to* EPHESIA. *She holds it for a moment, opens the door to the kiln.*)

EPHESIA: Good-bye forever.

AVIS: Good-bye forever.

SLOAN: Good-bye forever.

(EPHESIA *throws the hat in the kiln, shuts the door. He hands her the skates. Once again, she opens the door to the kiln.)*

EPHESIA: Good-bye forever.

AVIS: Good-bye forever.

SLOAN: Good-bye forever.

(She throws the skates in the kiln, shuts the door. SLOAN *proffers the paper sack.)*

SLOAN: I got you something.

EPHESIA: What is it?

SLOAN: Monkey flower.

(She opens the bag and removes a revolver, turns it in her hand, shows the revolver to AVIS. *He touches it, turns it in his hand, gives it back to* EPHESIA.*)*

AVIS: Where'd you get that?

SLOAN: Mailman brought it to me...you can make people disappear with that thing.

*(*EPHESIA *opens the door, considers the revolver in her hand for a moment, and then shuts the door. She places it back in the paper sack and keeps it.* AVIS *reaches into his pocket and removes two more nickels. He gives one to* EPHESIA *and they put the nickels into* SLOAN's *ears.* SLOAN *touches them and smiles.)*

SLOAN: Chickenshit fuckface monkeydick vaginaballs...

SLOAN, AVIS & EPHESIA: Buttfuck on the window

(Lights come up in the dining room. AMOS *enters from* RILTHE's *bedroom. He is bare-chested and there are pheasant feathers adorned in his hair. He carries the black medical bag, crosses through the living room, exits up the stairs. From somewhere in the house a horrible moaning can be heard. It grows louder as lights fade to black.)*

Scene Three

(SMALLWOOD *enters through the front door. The living room is empty. He slowly looks around, touches the surfaces of things. Moments later,* EPHESIA *enters holding a bowl of glaze and* AMOS' *wooden pin. Her walking is slow and deliberate and suggests weakness.*)

SMALLWOOD: Hello Ephesia.

EPHESIA: Hi.

SMALLWOOD: How are you today?

EPHESIA: Fine. (*She crosses to the table, sits, starts to mix the bowl of glaze with the wooden pin.*)

SMALLWOOD: Is your mother around?

EPHESIA: She's out with Amos.

(*He points to the bowl of glaze.*)

SMALLWOOD: Working hard?

EPHESIA: Uh-huh.

SMALLWOOD: Good, good.

(*He offers her a stick of gum from his pocket. She accepts it.*)

EPHESIA: What are you doing here?

SMALLWOOD: I was just in the neighborhood. Had an appointment with Father Bob over at Saint Catherine's. They need some fixtures for their choir loft. I thought I'd come by to see how you were.

EPHESIA: It won't stop.

SMALLWOOD: Would you like to go for a ride with me? Talk a little?

EPHESIA: Talk about what?

SMALLWOOD: Oh, I don't know. Pheasants. Archery. How you're feeling... I'd like to help you, Ephesia. I could take you to the hospital. No one would have to know.

(He holds his hand out to her. She stands very still.)

SMALLWOOD: It would be our little secret.

(She crosses to the sofa, reaches underneath the sofa, removes the paper bag containing the revolver, crosses back to SMALLWOOD very slowly, pushing off the table. She considers his hand for a moment, takes it, and they exit.)

(Moments later, SLOAN enters from the staircase with a bloody bed sheet draped around his neck. He crosses the dining room and exits out the front door. Moments later he re-enters carrying the statue of Saint Anthony.)

(RILTHE enters from the front door with the bloody bed sheet. The bowl of glaze is still on the table. She looks at the bowl, confused. SLOAN appears from under the stairs, tries to sneak away.)

RILTHE: What have you done, Sloan? Where's Saint Anthony?

SLOAN: I took him for a walk.

RILTHE: Dear Jesus. A walk where?

SLOAN: Not far.

RILTHE: *(Holding up the sheet)* And why on earth did you hang this over the porch?

SLOAN: It's like a flag.

RILTHE: You're an idiot!

(He starts to walk toward her with the walker raised over his head.)

RILTHE: Stop where you are, Sloan!

(He stops.)

RILTHE: Now put that walker down this instant.

(He sets the walker down.)

RILTHE: What in God's name has gotten into you?

SLOAN: I used to live down here. *(Pointing to various places in the dining room)* I lived in this room. And that room. And the other room. And the bathroom. And in your room.

RILTHE: Yes you did, Sloan. But now my room is off limits.

SLOAN: Amos gets to live in there.

RILTHE: Sloan, you're upstairs because we want you to be closer to God. A closer proximity to divinity fosters the healing process and eases suffering. That's why Chick stays on the upper story.

SLOAN: There's something missing here. Too many spaces. Like the wind's blowin in your stomach.

RILTHE: Nothing is missing, Sloan.

SLOAN: Like it's snowin inside you.

RILTHE: You're just tired and you need to rest. If you're going to heal properly you can't be coming down here all the time.

SLOAN: Amos is down here all the time. He lives down here.

RILTHE: That's because he's supervising things now. He's just filling in during your recovery... And why on earth are there coins in your ears?

SLOAN: Cause I'm in the club.

RILTHE: What club?

SLOAN: Coins in Your Ears Club. Just became a member.

RILTHE: And how does one become a member?

SLOAN: Oh, you can't join. They gotta invite you. Chickenshit fuckface monkeydick vaginaballs—

RILTHE: I wish you would go back upstairs, Sloan. And I don't want to continue having these ridiculous conversations, is that understood?

SLOAN: Can I have my walker back?

RILTHE: I thought you didn't need it anymore.

SLOAN: I like carryin it.

(She gives it back to him.)

RILTHE: Good night, Sloan.

(SLOAN exits up the stairs, carrying his walker.)

(AMOS enters from the front door hauling an enormous crucifix wrapped in brown paper. He is bare-chested. He carries the crucifix on his back and it takes a great effort. RILTHE clears things out of the way. He props it up against the wall.)

(RILTHE turns to AMOS, wipes his chest with the bed sheet.)

(Lights fade.)

Scene Four

(That evening. SLOAN is seated in the living room next to a display table. He is polishing a cross.)

(SMALLWOOD is seated on the sofa, although the lights and his demeanor should suggest a different location. He is holding an astrology book. A large suitcase and his briefcase are set at his feet. EPHESIA is behind him, folding an enormous heap of laundry.)

SMALLWOOD: *(Reading aloud from a book)* I once observed and overheard a meeting between a girl Archer and a man with a Scorpio Ascendant. At the time they were

introduced, she was about fifteen, and typically
believed she was going to remain in that glowing
chronological niche forever. He was soft-spoken and
intelligent, perhaps three decades or so her senior. A
quiet man, of distinguished appearance, who wore
glasses and whose hair line was lightly receding. He
was completely kind and courteous to her when they
were introduced, but shortly afterward, she turned to
her companion and whispered, "He's really proof of life
after death, isn't he?" Then she exploded into peals of
laughter in appreciation of their own cleverness.

Astrology often takes an amused, tolerant view of
Sagittarian's ability to kill with a word, but there are
times when the frankness of a Sag—

EPHESIA:*(Correcting his mispronunciation)* Sag. Like a "J".

SMALLWOOD: Of course, *Sag. (Back to the book)* ...but
there are times when the frankness of a *Sag* exceeds the
boundaries of sensitivity and good taste, and can be
described as nothing short of inhuman and indecent
cruelty. Now and then, these Archers need a slap of
truth themselves. A sharp slap.

Fortunately, most Sagittarian women are the kind
whose Jupiter rulership causes them to spread more
joy and sunlight than pain .And it's this type of *Sadge*
who can truly bless an Eagle with their holly-berry
personality Symbolized by the Centaur (half horse,
half human), she sometimes stumbles clumsily, and
sometimes glides gracefully into his life, trailing
brightly colored streamers of hope and optimism.
Her contagiously cheerful smile flashes into the
dark corners of his soul like a remembered song
from a happier time, and lights up his buried dreams,
resurrecting them with the promise of new life.
(He closes the book.)

EPHESIA: *(Perturbed)* Mister Smallwood, do you like
your shirts folded or on hangers?

SMALLWOOD: Whatever's easier, Ephesia. And please call me Lorenzo.

EPHESIA: Lorenzo.

SMALLWOOD: Or Zoe.

EPHESIA: Zoe... *(Sarcastic, folding shirts)* Some motel.

SMALLWOOD: Now, now, Ephesia, let's try and appreciate what God has granted us.

EPHESIA: They don't even have a pool. Or video games.

SMALLWOOD: Have you taken your medicine yet?

(She nods.)

SMALLWOOD: Doctor said you should be as good as new in a couple weeks.

EPHESIA: When are you gonna take me to the mountains?

SMALLWOOD: In due time, Ephesia. In due time.

EPHESIA: When's that?

SMALLWOOD: When I get to know you a little better.

EPHESIA: What do you want to know?

SMALLWOOD: Oh, just things. Things about you. Things about your family.

EPHESIA: What about my family?

SMALLWOOD: Oh I don't know. About your brothers.

EPHESIA: What about my brothers.

(AMOS and RILTHE enter the living room. AMOS is holding a hair brush. Like SLOAN, AMOS and RILTHE are unaware of EPHESIA and SMALLWOOD, and vice versa. RILTHE and AMOS sit at the dining room table. AMOS brushes RILTHE's hair over the following:)

EPHESIA: What do you want to know?

SMALLWOOD: Oh, just the general stuff. Tell me about Amos.

EPHESIA: He used to be a fireman

SMALLWOOD: What else?

EPHESIA: He was kicked out of the firehouse.

SMALLWOOD: Why's that?

EPHESIA: Because he broke some rules.

SMALLWOOD: What kind of rules?

EPHESIA: He let some people burn.

SMALLWOOD: Well, that happens sometimes.

EPHESIA: To death.

SMALLWOOD: Huh.

EPHESIA: A whole family.

SMALLWOOD: Maybe it was an accident.

EPHESIA: He locked em in.

SMALLWOOD: Why would he do something like that?

EPHESIA: They were mongrels.

SMALLWOOD: Mongrels?

EPHESIA: That's what Mother calls them. Mongrels, mutts and half-breeds.

SMALLWOOD: Well, maybe he couldn't help them.

EPHESIA: What's that supposed to mean?

SMALLWOOD: Maybe it was too late.

EPHESIA: It wasn't too late. He was in the room with them.

SMALLWOOD: How do you know?

EPHESIA: Because he took something.

SMALLWOOD: From their home?

EPHESIA: He takes it up to the attic. In front of Chick's room. He goes there to hide with it. I'm the only one who knows.

SMALLWOOD: Why in front of Chick's room?

EPHESIA: Because no one goes up there.

SMALLWOOD: Huh... Well, what does he do with it?

EPHESIA: He brushes it.

SMALLWOOD: Brushes what?

EPHESIA: Hair.

SMALLWOOD: *Hair?*

EPHESIA: From a little girl.

SMALLWOOD: A piece of it? ...A lock?

EPHESIA: No, the whole thing.

SMALLWOOD: The whole thing.

EPHESIA: It's long and black. There's a barrette in it. He keeps it in it so the bangs don't fall. It's the kind of black hair that you can see a mile away.

SMALLWOOD: Must be an awfully pretty head of hair.

EPHESIA: You can see where the head was.

SMALLWOOD: The head?

EPHESIA: Yep. He brushes it until it shines. And then he cleans himself with it.

SMALLWOOD: The bones of men are filled with tricky marrow.

EPHESIA: Want to know anything else?

SMALLWOOD: Huh?

EPHESIA: I asked if you wanted to know anything else.

SMALLWOOD: Oh. No. No, that's enough for today. Come here and rub my shoulders.

(She steps over the pile of clothes and starts to massage his neck and shoulders. AMOS *continues brushing* RILTHE's *hair.)*

EPHESIA: I want our cabin to have a garden in the back.

SMALLWOOD: Oh, that's good, Ephesia.

EPHESIA: A garden with flowers and vegetables and berries. And I want the bumblebees and the butterflies to do somersaults in the air. And the bears and the cougars and the mountain lions will come and eat the berries and play tag and protect the flowers. And they'll make stools there for fertilizer. And everything will grow twice as much.

SMALLWOOD: A little to the left, Ephesia.

EPHESIA: And we'll set up a big target in the back yard. And I'll practice my archery every day so if anyone ever comes to bother us we'll shoot em dead.

*(*AMOS *stops combing* RILTHE's *hair, exits.)*

SMALLWOOD: Sounds good to me.

EPHESIA: And we'll have a room where we'll keep the pheasants. I'll catch em and you can feed em. We'll build little beds for them to sleep in. With little pillows. And we'll have to have a big window in the room so they can look out and see the sky. They'll need something to look out at. It'll be like our own little family.

SMALLWOOD: A little to the right, Ephesia. A little to the right.

(She continues to massage him as lights simultaneously fade in the living and dining rooms.)

Scene Five

*(RILTHE is seated at the dining room table. AMOS enters
from the stairwell, holding one high top basketball sneaker.)*

RILTHE: Well?

AMOS: He stopped screamin.

RILTHE: Where's the other shoe?

AMOS: I could only get one.

RILTHE: He's half your size, Amos.

AMOS: He kept kickin me.

RILTHE: I hope you realize that you're floundering very
badly, Amos. Floundering like some pathetic trout on
a sidewalk. Such humiliation at the hands of a child.
It's becoming quite embarrassing.

(AMOS starts to cry.)

RILTHE: Get yourself together! How dare you pity
yourself! You are not a toddler! Don't be such a
mockery... How much of the game had he played
when you found him?

AMOS: Half.

RILTHE: I suppose you had to chase him though the
bleachers.

AMOS: I caught him!

RILTHE: I'm sure he put up a fierce fight. All
seventy-five pounds of him.

AMOS: I had to run through the whole damn locker
room. All them little faggots in their monkey suits.
Some nigger kid tried trippin me.

RILTHE: Sounds like there was plenty of team spirit. Esprit de corps... Is he still in that silly uniform?

AMOS: He aint' takin it off.

RILTHE: And he still doesn't know where his sister is.

AMOS: No, ma'am.

RILTHE: When he comes down I want to be alone with him. Go sweep the neighborhood one more time. Take the floodlight from the garage.

AMOS: Yes ma'am.

(AMOS *exits. The sound of someone descending the stairs can be heard. It tops.* RILTHE *polishes a cross.*)

RILTHE: Avis, if that's you, I'd advise you to gather some courage and face this like a man. Holing up in your room all night isn't going to do anything but make the punishment sting more once it's administered. The salt only gets saltier. If you ever plan on becoming a man, the time to correct you coward's posture and thicken the moxy in your blood is now.

(*She continues her polishing. More descending footfalls*)

RILTHE: Whatever's happened to the men in this family is a mystery to me. We have your father's broken faculties and now you and your cowardly defiance. What's happened to the men? Cowardice and imbecility. Tumorous flaws invading my house. Like some kind of malignant pollen slipping through the cracks. Time to caulk the windows again. Tighten the hinges. Bones are supposed to grow stronger with age, not crumble. Cowardice and imbecility...

(AVIS *appears from the stairwell. He is wearing a basketball uniform that is too large. He also wears one high-top basketball sneaker and one jumping shoe. His wrists have been slashed and blood drips off his fingertips. He stands*

behind RILTHE. *She continues to polish crosses as lights fade*
to black.)

Scene Six

(The hospital room: somewhere in the house. It is a stark
white room with a large cross on the wall opposite the bed.
There is a small porthole-like window oddly positioned on one
wall. It is too high for a child to look out of. Light streams
through the window. AVIS *is sleeping in a bed. There is a*
pitcher of water with a large flexible straw placed on a table
near his head. RILTHE *is seated at the side of the bed, holding*
a Bible. From the living room, AMOS *ascends the stairs,*
carrying two white leather straps. There is a Rosary wrapped
around one of her hands. AMOS *enters, pulls* AVIS' *hands*
over his head and ties them to the corners of the bed. AVIS'
wrists and forearms are stained with blood. AMOS *exits.*
RILTHE *watches* AVIS *sleep and then slowly reaches out to*
place her hand on his forehead, but retracts it. He wakes.)

RILTHE: I've prayed to God, Avis. I've been sitting
here praying for five hours now. I've prayed aloud.
I've prayed in song. And I've prayed privately.
With the silent voice that God places inside of you.
The voice he reserves for tragedy and spiritual affliction.
I've prayed until the sentences and the words and
the syllables have collapsed and lost their meaning.
I haven't eaten or slept or taken water. I have only
prayed.
   I need to understand this, Avis. To understand why
a Klieg would entertain such a base and egotistical
notion. I've seen dogs maul their stomachs out.
I've seen birds fly into the sides of windowless
buildings. Once I even saw an alley cat jump in front
of a riding mower. A full sprint for the blades.
Lemmings rarely get through a lifetime without making
a death dive. It's common knowledge that even the

dinosaurs threw themselves from the edges of cliffs. But you are not a beast, Avis. The shades of suicide don't reside in the anatomy of the well-adjusted human species. The murder of the self is the murder of God.

When I first saw what you had done, Avis, I actually thought that we had been blessed with a miracle. That god had visited upon our house. That your palms were marked with Stigmata. That the blood spilling on my floor was blessed with divinity. That your small and insignificant life had suddenly gained a special meaning. That you had been marked a Saint. St. Avis of the Slight and Feeble. The little boy saint with the coat size of a leper child. But I was wrong, Avis. My thoughts were no better than the blind, importunate scrawl of a forger's signature.

Even before you were born, Avis, I knew there would be weakness. I could feel it when I carried you. Your little mouse hands scrabbling in my womb. Your spindly legs folded at the knees like a locust's. Your blind little eyes rolled back like those of some sleeping rodent. The thing inside of me. That's what you became, Avis—the thing inside me.

And then there was your birth. Your cowardly retreat. You wouldn't even push yourself from the safety of my uterus. The doctors had to coax you out like some lazy, bloated tapeworm. The diameter of your head was too large, Avis. Your shoulders wouldn't turn. Despite the drugs. Despite the contractions that had caused my skin to stretch and tear. Despite the enormous gap your brother and sisters had left. So they cut you out. They sliced me open like a goat in a pasture.

I should have known early on yours would be a head full of spite and pride. The willful head of the Cyclops. Too heavy for the shoulders. Too immense. The head that didn't want to come out. Like a balloon full of glue. A trick balloon that wouldn't burst. Such selfishness even as an infant. Even in the womb.

We had you late because we thought you would be
perfect. With each child your father and I made
progress. First there was Chick. A disaster. Her face
folded into itself like some pink and freakish
cauliflower. Then God gave us Amos. A man-child who
could split wood and lift the corners of cars, but failed
to learn his math tables. Couldn't spell himself out of a
phone booth. And things kept getting better with your
sister. Her beauty and her intelligence and the
symmetry of her structure. But all of that along with the
defiance and the ambition and the will of a bridge
builder. And now you. A regression.

(CHICK *appears at the foot of* AVIS' *bed. She is seen only by*
AVIS. *Over her head she wears a pillow sack with a child's
ghost face drawn on the front. She sits at the foot of the bed
and reaches out and starts to gently stroke* AVIS'*s feet.*)

RILTHE: A boy stopped by to see you today, Avis. A
Negro. A tall, anthropoidal Negro. His skin a strange,
deep shade of black. A medicine black. Almost blue.
Color of spoiled fruit. Buck-toothed. Lips from a mule's
mouth. Bow-legged and pigeon-toed. Looked like one
of those degenerates from the reformatory. He walked
onto our porch and knocked on our door. The nerve of
a drunken sailor.
    He was holding a bouquet of flowers, Avis. I thought
he was bringing them to your sister. Or to me for that
matter. A primate on a flower run. Skimmed from
the probation pond. The local nursery has been known
to hire such flotsam. Looks good. Keeps the romantics
in line during the holidays. Look at our darkies, aren't
they savage-like roaming in the ivy? I thought he
was one of their runners or jumpers or gatherers or
whatever they use them for. But he introduces himself.
He tells me his name. Sample. The names they come
up with anymore. Misspelled cars. Things you read on
menus. Phonetic perversions. Sample. Like something

copied off of a cardboard box.

So he holds out his flowers, Avis. In all of his crooked
ineptitude, he holds them out with the conviction of a
blind dog that smells food in a room. And he says they
are for you. He says that he bought them himself and
that they are for you.

They were the kind of flowers that a man gives to a
woman, Avis. Red roses. A dozen of them. A lover's
dozen. He said they were for you.

(AVIS *tries to reach the straw again and fails.* CHICK *rises off
the bed and moves the straw closer to his mouth. He drinks
while she strokes the crown of his head.)*

RILTHE: When you regain your strength, Avis, you'll
have some explaining to do. About a great many things.
If you know the whereabouts of your sister you will tell
me. God put a voice in your throat and you will use it.
This family will not be blighted by the invisible worms
you and your sister have plotted. The bone either grows
thicker or it emaciates.

(RILTHE *falls silent as* CHICK *continues to stroke* AVIS' *feet.
Lights fade.)*

Scene Seven

(*The dining room.* SLOAN *is draping his blue suit over the
arms of the giant crucifix, seemingly trying to dress it.
He is wearing his worker's clothes and* EPHESIA's *blood-
stained smock. He moves slowly to the head of the table,
sits, starts to polish a stack of crosses.)*

(*The light changes slightly.* EPHESIA *enters very quietly
through the front door. Her clothes are slightly more
sophisticated and she perhaps wears makeup. She is
shivering.* SMALLWOOD *follows with an enormous box.
He sets the box down in the center of the floor.* SLOAN *is*

*completely unaware of their presence and continues to slowly
wipe down the crosses.)*

EPHESIA: Where are we?

SMALLWOOD: Why, we're here.

EPHESIA: What's with all the sand?

SMALLWOOD: This is the desert. Look at that sky!
(pointing) There's the arrow from Orion's bow! And
there, over there, is Antares, the heart of the Scorpion.
And there, his deadly tail. Such celestial beauty,
Ephesia. Don't you think?

EPHESIA: Where's my mountain?

SMALLWOOD: In due time, Ephesia, in due time. *(He
reaches into the box and starts to remove the ceramic crosses
that he had purchased, makes a pattern on the floor with the
crosses, using the entire dining room.)*

EPHESIA: What are you doing?

SMALLWOOD: Ephesia, some things aren't so easily seen
at first. One must have faith.

EPHESIA: Why are we in the desert?

SMALLWOOD: Because sand is a symbol of history
and providence. It can take the shape of many things.
Many, many things.

EPHESIA: What are you talking about?

SMALLWOOD: I'm talking about God's great migrating
mountain, Ephesia. Soon you shall see.

EPHESIA: See where?

SMALLWOOD: It will just be suddenly there. The way
all things good are arrived at. Just so suddenly there.
Be patient, Ephesia.

EPHESIA: I want to go back to the Holy Van. I'm thirsty.

(Suddenly, lights come up in the hospital room. AMOS is standing before AVIS' bed. In one hand he holds a bouquet of red roses. In the other a bedpan. AVIS sleeps deeply.)

SMALLWOOD: Only God can truly quench the breath of the beleaguered.

EPHESIA: Well then I want to talk to God cause you're acting really weird.

(SMALLWOOD continues to create his pattern. We can see that it is starting to take the shape of an enormous cross.)

SMALLWOOD: *(Finishing the pattern)* Ephesia, when God created love he intended that love to be contained inside the body *(Finishing the cross)* The human body is simply an empty cavity until it is filled. An empty, rueful cavity. But once each body is filled with this love, there is a sudden harmony. A sense of sublime completion. A feeling of divine inevitability. And it's white. Like holy, angelic light. It's hot and it's blinding and it's white.
   God intends all creatures to celebrate the joy of the creation of this love, Ephesia. Adam and Eve celebrated this love. And although Jesus never lain with another, he contained this love in his body. In his hands and in his eyes and in his breath.

(In the hospital room, AMOS places the roses in the bed pan, takes a lighter out of his pocket and sets them on fire.)

EPHESIA: Why are there feathers in your hair?

SMALLWOOD: Are there feathers in my hair?

EPHESIA: There are pheasant feathers all over your hair.

SMALLWOOD: I don't have anything in my hair, Ephesia.

EPHESIA: Where's my mountain?!

SMALLWOOD: Settle down, Ephesia. Settle down.

EPHESIA: *(Producing the revolver)* What did the wolf say to the chicken?

(SMALLWOOD hesitates, puts his arms up.)

EPHESIA: He says What fine feathers you have.

SMALLWOOD: Okay.

EPHESIA: Say it.

SMALLWOOD: What fine feathers you have.

EPHESIA: And how did the chicken reply?

SMALLWOOD: I don't know, Ephesia.

EPHESIA: He says Thank you Mister Wolf...

SMALLWOOD: Please put the gun down.

EPHESIA: Do it!

SMALLWOOD: Thank you Mister Wolf...

EPHESIA: Thank you Mister Wolf would you like to see where I lay my eggs.

SMALLWOOD: Thank you Mister Wolf would you like to see where I lay my eggs.

(EPHESIA fires, hits SMALLWOOD.)

EPHESIA: Beep beep. *(She fires again.)* Beep beep. *(She fires again.)* Beep beep.

(SMALLWOOD falls in the center of the giant cross he had patterned. EPHESIA stands there for a moment, drops the gun, and runs off.)

(In the dining room, the light returns to its setting at the beginning of the scene.)

(RILTHE enters from the front door, sees SLOAN's blue suit hanging on the crucifix. She quickly moves to the crucifix and pulls the blue suit off of it. She starts to fold it angrily. SLOAN starts to pick up the desert crosses, stacks them in the box left by SMALLWOOD.)

SLOAN: I had a dream about your hair.

RILTHE: Is that right?

SLOAN: Uh-huh.

RILTHE: You had a picture?

SLOAN: Funny little dream

RILTHE: I'm sure it was funny, Sloan. Funny as the grin
of a moron.

SLOAN: There was all this noise. Loudest thing I ever
heard. Like a train was comin. We were strangers but I
knew it was you. Cause I could smell you. I could smell
your hair. Like I remember it on your pillow. The way it
smelled like rain on your pillow. And that train noise
was getting louder and louder. And I couldn't figure it
out. Cause it was just you and me. So I walked over
to you. Real close. Closer than I've ever been. And I
realized that it was your *voice* makin the train noise.
I tried to close your mouth but it wouldn't shut.
So I made your hair disappear. With a big old bowie
knife. Worked real nice. Kept your hair all in one piece,
too. Then I squeezed it into a little ball and I stuffed
it in you mouth. And that train noise stopped. It was
so quiet it sounded like the room was breathing.
You coulda heard a penny fallin on the moon.

RILTHE: Sloan, if this doesn't stop I will put you back in
the hospital. I have spoken with the doctors. They are
aware of your regressions and they're willing to take
you back. Just keep it up.

(SLOAN *exits with the box of crosses.*)

(*Lights fade.*)

Scene Eight

(Later that evening. The dining room. The crucifix has been secured on the wall, below the stained glass window. RILTHE *stands before it. She wipes it with a cloth.* AMOS *enters from the front door.)*

RILTHE: So?

AMOS: No one's seen her.

RILTHE: Did you try downtown?

AMOS: Every bowling alley, doughnut shop and train station. Nothin.

RILTHE: She just upped and vanished. The Great Vanishing Klieg. I didn't know magicians ran in the family...is the hole filled?

AMOS: No ma'am.

RILTHE: Well, why not?

AMOS: It's gone.

RILTHE: What's gone?

AMOS: The body.

RILTHE: The body's gone!

AMOS: It ain't in the freezer.

RILTHE: Well, where in God's name is it? It didn't just up and walk away.

AMOS: It was there last night.

RILTHE: You've failed me twice now, Amos.
In succession. You must like failure. I imagine
that it tastes good in your mouth. Like a blackberry.
A fresh, ripe blackberry. It must be delicious.

(AMOS *sits on the floor. He pulls* CHICK's *pillowcase out of his pocket, pulls it over his head, cries.*)

AMOS: I'll find it.

RILTHE: You'd better believe you'll find it! The last thing we need is your father carting it around in some godforsaken wheelbarrow or some such thing. A little parade for the neighbors. Why don't we just knock on their doors and give them handfuls confetti to throw.

(RILTHE *pulls the pillow case off his head.* AMOS *hides his face for a moment, then stands, his hands behind his back.*)

RILTHE: Is there anything else I should know?

AMOS: The kiln's busted

RILTHE: What do you mean, busted.

AMOS: It overheated.

RILTHE: Well how on earth did that happen?

AMOS: Father overloaded it.

RILTHE: Overloaded it with what?

AMOS: Saint Anthony.

RILTHE: Saint Anthony! (*She crosses to the front door and looks at the front porch. She slams the door.*) Well that's just...fucked!

(*Pause*)

AMOS: Cross looks good.

RILTHE: Of course it looks good.

(*Lights fade*)

Scene Nine

(Split scene. The basement and the hospital room.)

(In the hospital room AVIS *is sleeping. His hands and wrists are still bandaged.* EPHESIA *enters very quietly through the window. She moves to the side of the bed and takes his hand.)*

EPHESIA: Chickenshit... *(No response)* ...Chickenshit fuckface... *(No response)* Chickenshit... *(No response)* Avis... Earth to Avis.

(He wakes.)

EPHESIA: What's up, G?

(They stare at each other for a moment.)

AVIS: You missed my game.

EPHESIA: I know. I'm sorry.

AVIS: I made three baskets. Set things up. Ran the offense.

(In the basement, SLOAN *stands in front of the kiln, beside* CHICK's *corpse, which he has set in a chair. The statue of Saint Anthony has been forced into the mouth of the kiln.* CHICK's *corpse is crudely manipulated into a seated position. The back of the head, which is covered with a pillow case, faces the audience.)*

AVIS: Where were you?

EPHESIA: Away.

AVIS: Away where?

EPHESIA: Just away.

(In the basement, SLOAN *removes some nickels from his bag of change. He puts nickels in his own ears. He then crosses to* CHICK's *corpse and inserts two nickels into either ear.)*

EPHESIA: Avis, before I left I talked to Chick. Through
the slot. She took the pillowcase off. I could see the
parts in her face. They looked like vegetables. Beautiful
vegetables. Green beans and lettuce and cauliflowers.
Tomatoes and carrots. Her face was like a garden.

*(In the basement, CHICK's ghost appears out of the shadows.
She wears the ghost face pillow case over her head. She moves
to SLOAN and takes his hand in hers. She lifts his hand and
guides it under the opening of the pillow case.)*

EPHESIA: She painted cities on her walls, Avis. Each
wall was a different city. Buildings and chain link
fences and people. She used all of these colors. It was
like you were there. Even through the slot it was like
that.

AVIS: What cities?

EPHESIA: She said they were different cities where the
Jews lived. And there was one all the way in the back
that wasn't like the other cities. I don't even think it was
a city. There were all these people flying. Really skinny
people. Some were really old and some were just little
kids. You could see their ribs and the bones in their
hands. And they were naked. And even though they
were so skinny they didn't look hungry. They looked
like they were happy. Like they were happy because
they were flying. The way angels are happy, Avis.
It was beautiful.

AVIS: What was it?

EPHESIA: Chick said it was Trueblinka. I think it's
another word for heaven.

AVIS: Trueblinka.

EPHESIA: It's a beautiful word isn't it?

(In the basement, footfalls can be heard descending the stairs. CHICK's *ghost disappears.* SLOAN *waves the heat toward* CHICK's *corpse.)*

EPHESIA: I slept in her room last night.

AVIS: You were here?

EPHESIA: I climbed up the vines.

AVIS: They didn't see you?

EPHESIA: I'm in and out so fast they don't even know. They can't touch me.

AVIS: They think you're going one way and then you're not there.

EPHESIA: You make yourself small.

AVIS: And they can't find you.

EPHESIA: Chick's gone, Avis. And the cities are gone, too. They painted over them. They painted the whole room white. Everything's gone.

(In the basement, the descending footfalls grow louder. SLOAN *tries to hide* CHICK's *corpse.)*

EPHESIA: Avis, you have to get out of here. They put your bed in Chick's room.

AVIS: Where am I supposed to go?

EPHESIA: I still have the Holy Van. We'll drive to the mountains.

AVIS: I gotta go back to school.

EPHESIA: You don't need school, Avis.

AVIS: Just for one day.

EPHESIA: For what?

AVIS: Sample. I want to say goodbye. He brought me flowers.

(In the basement AMOS appears with a bottle of pills.)

EPHESIA: I'll be here tomorrow night. At midnight. I'll honk three times. I'll park in the alley. If you get in any trouble my bow is under the sofa.

AVIS: What about your monkeyflower gun?

EPHESIA: I left it.

AVIS: Left it where?

EPHESIA: Away.

(In the basement, AMOS forces the pills on SLOAN. SLOAN tries to insert them into the mouth of CHICK's corpse. AMOS intercepts them and forces them into SLOAN's mouth.)

AVIS: I'm tired.

EPHESIA: Go to sleep.

AVIS: I dream about him, Ephesia... He says, "Pass the rock, G. Pass the rock".

EPHESIA: Shshshsh.*(Caressing his head)* Tomorrow night. Three honks. Don't forget.

(AVIS nods, falls asleep. EPHESIA moves the bedside table under the window, pulls herself up, and exits through the window. Lights fade in the hospital room.)

(Lights fade in the basement.)

Scene Ten

(The following day. The attic. CHICK's bedroom. The only piece of furniture is a pair of small twin cots. The walls are whitewashed. There is a large steel door with a slot, and a small window, similar in style to the window in the hospital room. A bedpan rests in the corner. SLOAN sits on one of the beds. He is wearing his worker's uniform. His leg is manacled to the frame of the cot. He stares off. Keys jingle, the bolt

turns and the steel door opens. RILTHE *enters.* AMOS *follows behind her, pushing* AVIS *in front of him.* AVIS' *hands are still heavily bandaged. He is dressed in a hospital gown.* AMOS *exits.* RILTHE *stands in the doorway for a moment and then she turns and exits. Keys turn and the steel door locks.* AVIS *and* SLOAN *sit in silence for a moment.* AVIS *stands and looks out the window.)*

SLOAN: They're makin a hole for you...I got a bowie knife on my leg. It'll cut just about anything.

AVIS: I'm climbing down the ivy.

SLOAN: It ain't there no more. Amos cut it down this morning.

*(*AVIS *crosses to the window, looks out.)*

AVIS: I'll tie the sheets together.

SLOAN: Where you gonna go?

AVIS: The mountains.

SLOAN: Monkey flower country. Cold up there. Snow gets bigger than you.

AVIS: We're gonna live in a cabin. Make a garden.

SLOAN: If you let me come with you I'll protect you.

AVIS: You can't fit through there.

*(*AVIS *bends down and raises* SLOAN's *pant leg and removes an enormous bowie knife. He starts to saw the chain attached to his manacle.)*

SLOAN: I can make myself pretty small. Been practicin every day. You'd be surprised. You just close your eyes and picture a butterfly. The wings and all the colors. You picture it just sittin there. Right on the window sill. When that picture starts to look real nice you make all the air leave your body and you put the butterfly inside you. Right in the old stomach. It ain't hard once you get

the hang of it. I can make myself smaller than you
sometimes. Smaller than most things.

(SLOAN *reaches under his T-shirt, removes a necklace of
dried ears, places it over* AVIS' *head.* AVIS *touches the ears,
hands the bowie knife back to* SLOAN. AVIS *moves to his bed
and rips his sheets off. He hands them to* SLOAN. SLOAN
*begins knotting the sheets together. When he is finished he
hands one end of the sheet to* AVIS, *who ties it around his
waist.* SLOAN *ties his end around his waist.* AVIS *mounts the
sill, starts to crawl through the window, turns back.*)

SLOAN: Chickenshit.

AVIS: Chickenshit.

(AVIS *starts to pass through the window as lights fade.*)

Scene Eleven

(*Very late that evening. The dining room. A church choir
plays on the phonograph.* RILTHE *wipes down the display
tables.*)

(SLOAN *enters from the staircase. He is naked.*
RILTHE *turns, startled.*)

RILTHE: How long have you been standing there, Sloan?

SLOAN: For about forty years.

RILTHE: Who let you out?

SLOAN: I did.

RILTHE: Where's your uniform?

SLOAN: It fell off when I made myself small.

RILTHE: I will not tolerate your games tonight, Sloan.
What happened to your chains?

SLOAN: He made em disappear.

RILTHE: Who made em disappear?

SLOAN: My roommate.

RILTHE: Avis couldn't make salt vanish in the wind.

SLOAN: He made em disappear and then he crawled out the window.

RILTHE: And I suppose you turned into a mouse and ran through the vents.

SLOAN: I don't know how to do that yet. I can do a butterfly but I can't do no mouse.

RILTHE: What do you want, Sloan?

SLOAN: Why are you makin a hole for Avis?

RILTHE: There was a time when you would've dug the hole yourself, Sloan.

SLOAN: He's just a boy.

RILTHE: He is a weakling! And you're an imbecile! This Great Line of Klieg Men! Marring the gene pool! Polluting our heritage!

(He holds the bowie knife in front of him.)

SLOAN: Winter's comin.

RILTHE: Put that away, Sloan.

(He doesn't move.)

RILTHE: Sloan, you give that to me this instant!

(She crosses to him angrily. He forces his hand over her mouth. The phonograph is jarred and starts to skip.)

SLOAN: I got trains inside of my voice, too. Big shiny ones. Louder than the ocean.

(He forces her to the basement stairs. They exit.)

(Moments later, AVIS enters in a rush from the front door. He is out of breath and panicked, the necklace of dried ears dangling outside of his shirt. He sprints for the sofa, reaches under it, removes EPHESIA's bow. AMOS enters. He is

wearing SLOAN's *blue suit. His head is covered with*
CHICK's *pillowcase and he is holding a shovel. His arms are*
dirty with mud. Behind him it is snowing. AMOS *takes a step*
toward AVIS. AVIS *draws back on the vacant bow.* SLOAN
enters from the basement. He is holding RILTHE's *scalped*
hair. He looks at AVIS *and* AMOS, *starts to weep.* AVIS
continues to draw back on the bow.)

(Three honks can be heard in the distance.)

(Blackout)

END OF PLAY

www.ingramcontent.com/pod-product-compliance
Lightning Source LLC
Chambersburg PA
CBHW052158090426
42741CB00010B/2320